5/20/14

MW00744678

Another Typical Cleveland Experience

(and other tales of a baseball junkie)

by

Wayne Pearsall

To Veronica who sees everything over my shoulder,

Hope you like my book,
My Best Always,
Go Tribe!

Copyright © 2014 by Midnight Mermaid LLC All photography in
this book was shot by the author or are part of the author's collection
unless another source is noted.

ISBN: 978-0-991084-1-2

All rights reserved. No part of this publication may be reproduced,
stored in a retrieval system or transmitted, in any form, or by any
means, electronic, mechanical, recorded, photocopied, or otherwise,
without the prior written permission of both the copyright owner and
the above publisher of this book, except by a reviewer who may
quote brief passages in a review.

The scanning, uploading, and distribution of this book via the Internet
or via any other means without the permission of the publisher is
illegal and punishable by law. Please purchase only authorized
electronic editions and do not participate in or encourage electronic
piracy of copyrightable materials. Your support of the author's rights
is appreciated.

Printed in the United States of America

Table of Contents

Dedicated to

Bernice Lorraine Gordon Pearsall

May she rest in peace

1922-2011

To my niece Nancy to whom I dedicate this
quote:

"A mistake is always forgivable,
rarely excusable and always unacceptable."

Robert Fripp

...thanks for forgiving me.

Love, Uncle Wayne

Acknowledgements

There are a number of people who assisted me in the production of this book and I want to take this opportunity to thank them. Joseph F. Gustin, an author himself, proofread early drafts of this book and also provided me with counsel, encouragement and suggestions from his knowledge of this business.

As the book came closer to becoming a finished project, Danielle Kawalek Trahan, court reporting instructor extraordinaire, proofread the book more than once and provided guidance on grammatical changes. I can't thank her enough for the quality of work she provided. Any grammatical errors in the book, therefore, are purely my responsibility.

I also want to thank fellow college instructors, John Mazi, Steve Kovacs and Katherine Miracle for the encouragement, guidance and suggestions that they provided.

Prologue

On a summer night many years ago I was driving through Georgia. I stopped at a hotel in suburban Atlanta which was on one of the many winding ribbons of highway that snake their way through Atlanta and would take me to an Atlanta Braves game later that evening at Fulton County Stadium.

After being told by the desk clerk the rate for a night, I told her it was too pricey. I started to leave and she offered me a room at a lower price. It was still too pricey but as the hotel appeared safe and clean, I agreed to the rate, checked in and went up to my room located on the top floor.

After cleaning up, I left for the Braves game. I punched the elevator button and got on the elevator with another guest. He and I started making small talk about our reasons for being in Atlanta when a woman and her young son stepped onto the elevator after it stopped on the next floor down. I had been telling the other guest that I was heading out to the ball game. "I'm a baseball junkie" were the next words out of my mouth.

The woman who just entered the elevator with her son abruptly hit a button on the elevator and nudged her son out into the adjacent hallway after the elevator door opened on the next floor.

Was she planning to get off on that floor anyway or did she forget something and decide to exit at the next floor to get back on an elevator to go back up to her room? Or was it my description of myself as a "junkie" that chased her and her son off the elevator.

The name of this book is "Another Typical Cleveland Experience." It was a statement another fan made after a tough Indians doubleheader loss at Cleveland Municipal Stadium. It was Friday night, July 27, 1990. I was living in Tampa at the time and took a short summer trip back to my hometown outside Cleveland to visit my Mom and Dad. Before the trip, I had just started dating a woman in Tampa who I was crazy about.

The Indians were hosting the Yankees in what used to be called a twilight night doubleheader. Two games in Cleveland between the Yankees and Indians were rained out early in the season and had to be rescheduled. One was added to the single game already scheduled on this Friday night and the other one was also scheduled on Sunday along with the regularly scheduled game. The teams would play five games against each other over the three days.

The Indians came into the game optimistic that they could win three, maybe four games, of the five game series. The Yankees were struggling with a 34-60 record. The Indians had a 46-50 record and a good series might give them some reason to be optimistic for the remainder of the season. Greg Swindell, the Indians left handed ace, would start the first game that night. Pitching against the Indians in that first game was Yankees left hand hurler, Andy Hawkins, who came into the game with a 1-8 Won Loss record.

The game was a pitchers duel and scoreless through six innings. In the top of the seventh inning, the Yankees first baseman, Steve Balboni, hit a solo home run to give the Yankees a 1-0 lead. In the top of the eighth inning, the Yankees center fielder, Roberto Kelly, hit a two run home run to give the Yankees a 3-0 lead. The Cleveland Indians would muster only three singles against Hawkins and not score any runs.

Andy Hawkins would improve his Won Loss record to 2-8 and his Earned Run Average would be lowered to 5.68. Swindell's record would drop to 6-6 and his earned run average would be 4.19 after the game. Steve Olin would pitch the last 1 1/3 innings of the game. A few years later, Olin would die in a boating accident during Spring Training in Florida. He was 27 when he passed away.

The game was over in less than two hours, a real baseball rarity. The Indians went on to lose the second game of the doubleheader 4-1. I remember a fan behind me, frustrated after the second loss; blurt out the words "another typical Cleveland experience." I am sure the 44,509 other fans agreed. I couldn't have said it better myself. The Indians would win the game against the Yankees on Saturday but lose both games of the Sunday doubleheader. I didn't go to those games. I thought I should spend some time with my Mom and Dad.

As I mentioned, before I left on this trip, I had started to date a young woman in Tampa that I was crazy about. While on this trip, I was looking forward to getting back to Tampa to see her. She was going to pick me up at the airport and, sure enough, she was there when my flight arrived.

The airlines managed to misplace one piece of my luggage. That extra time filling out forms and waiting for my luggage became terribly uncomfortable as the young woman that I was crazy about took that time to tell me that she started dating someone else while I was out of town.

In fact, she had something planned with her new boyfriend that evening and was kind of upset that she had to wait for me to fill out a claim form for my lost luggage. After I filled out the lost baggage form and getting assurances from the baggage clerk that my baggage would be delivered to my condominium the next day, my now ex-girlfriend drove me home.

She took me to my condominium in South Tampa and dropped me off. There I was, standing in the parking lot, watching her drive off and wondering if I would ever see her again. As I watched her drive off, I felt my heart drop into my stomach and thought about the words "another typical Cleveland experience."

I was numb and I really didn't want to go into my condo. After her car was completely out of sight, I dragged myself and my one suitcase up to my second floor unit. I unlocked the door, entered my unit which seemed emptier than usual, sat down and tried to make sense of what just happened.

I would think about her regularly for the next few months. I reached out to her on a few occasions only to be met with rejection. The emptiness that I felt plagued me for a while. One day, I remember waking up and thinking about her. Then I realized that I was just tired of dwelling on her. That was it, I didn't think about her much more after that.

There was some good news. I did see my luggage again; it was delivered the next day.

Preface

I started writing a book and its title was to be "Dead Husbands, Dead Ostriches and Baseball (or how I lived in Tampa for 25 years without having sex)." It was to be a book about my law practice and my life in Tampa but I started the book with the story about how I came to attend Game Six of the World Series in 1986 in New York City. After writing that story, I realized that it probably symbolized my life and any stories about me in the rest of the book would have been superfluous.

I also was concerned about violating my attorney-client privilege in telling some stories about my clients and getting the necessary releases from those clients and witnesses. For example, I represented the first woman to ever get the death penalty in Hillsborough County, Florida. Her name is Carla Caillier and the Florida Supreme Court subsequently reversed her death penalty and sentenced her to life imprisonment with no possibility of parole for at least 25 years. I do talk about that case in this book a little bit as there is a baseball story that goes with it.

The other case in the title referred to a client whose ostrich was frightened so much by the noise from an ascending hot air balloon that it ran in panic back and forth in its pen until it broke its legs and had to be put down. In the lawsuit, we alleged that the hot air balloon pilot allowed the balloon to get too close to the ground with the knowledge that the noise it would create from ascending would scare animals on the ground and possibly cause them to panic and be injured. Those were the two cases in my career that were reported in the local newspaper.

Instead of writing about my legal career and life in Tampa, I decided to write a book about baseball. I have read numerous baseball books and so many of them are very well written. After reading these books, I was inspired to write a book about my life and baseball. I can only hope this book can come close to meeting the benchmark set by so many great baseball authors.

A book not about baseball that I read while I was in Law School at Wayne State University in Detroit was "Zen and the Art of Motorcycle Maintenance: An Inquiry into Values" by Robert Pirsig. I owned a motorcycle myself and heeded the author's advice when I rode my motorcycle twice from Detroit to Florida and back.

The advice was to stay off the freeway and drive the old highways. By doing that, I was able to see the real America and meet real Americans for whom I have genuine affection. Although I no longer have a motorcycle, when I drive I try to stay off the freeway.

I think of my career as being on a freeway, practicing law and teaching law both in the Tampa and Cleveland areas. I think of going to baseball games as the times that I exit the freeway of my life and ride the old highways of America. As of the time I write this book, I have seen professional baseball at 89 different stadiums. I have seen baseball at its highest levels of excitement. I have also attended baseball games that just seemed to drag on endlessly.

I have also met many interesting people at these games and appreciate their affection, like mine, for this game of baseball. There are stories about me being heartbroken in this book. When compared to the tragedies and hardship of other people that I write about in this book, I realize how fortunate my life has been.

I hope you like this book about baseball and my life and that it inspires you to write a book too.

Introduction

Christmas, 1996. Every Christmas since I moved to Tampa in 1978, I traveled back to Lorain, Ohio, my birthplace, to visit my parents. They were divorced so I spent time with them separately. Lorain is 30 miles west of Cleveland and is located at the mouth of the Black River on Lake Erie. Lorain is far enough away from Cleveland not to be considered a suburb.

In 1996, my Mom still lived in the house where my parents brought me home from the hospital back in 1952. Dad owned a house in Lorain on the shores of Lake Erie.

On that trip, I also had occasion to drive into Cleveland. Cleveland Municipal Stadium was being demolished and I wanted to see it one more time. I had mixed feelings when I went by the stadium and saw it partially dismantled. Just like an old house or a favorite old car, the stadium had outlived its anticipated life span. It would have been easy to be nostalgic for this stadium where I spent time during my childhood and teenage years attending Indians and Browns games but I knew its time had come to be replaced. Besides, nobody lived there anymore, the most recent tenants, the Cleveland Browns, had vacated the place for a new home in Baltimore.

I was hoping to get a brick or something from the demolition as a keepsake of the times I spent there but the place was securely sealed off, probably to keep people like me from getting onto the property during the demolition. It was still sad to see the Stadium have to go through the process of being destroyed. I felt bad there couldn't have been a less tortuous way for it to be torn down. It deserved to be treated with more dignity but I'm not sure there is a dignified way to destroy stadiums.

Later that trip, I went to dinner with my Dad, his former secretary, Ruth, and her husband. After dinner, a discussion with Ruth and myself turned to what I had been doing on this trip and I told her about my drive by the stadium.

She asked me how I felt, seeing it being torn down. After telling her some of the emotions I mentioned above, I told her that some of my best memories of my childhood with my Dad were going to ballgames there with him.

Now, this book could be a story about how my Dad and I went to baseball games from my childhood until I became an adult and how these ballgames created a bonding between us. I could also talk about how going to these baseball games with my Dad was a metaphor of life and the transition to adulthood and passing on values from generation to generation.

I *do* remember fondly the times he took me to see the Cleveland Indians play during my childhood. Those games are easy to remember as there were only two of them. He would also take me to an All Star game in Cincinnati in 1970.

I was raised in the 1960s. To paraphrase Charles Dickens, to me the '60s were the "best of times and the worst of times, the age of foolishness and the epoch of belief." It was the time of the Vietnam War along with war protests, civil rights protests and riots in the cities. Yet, America did put a man on the moon.

Americans' taste in sports was transitioning from baseball to football. With the arrival of television, football became the sport of choice for Americans. Baseball, which does not translate well on television, especially compared to football, was losing popularity. In a football analogy, baseball was Johnny Unitas and football was Joe Namath.

It was a time of sex, drugs and rock and roll. Not for me though. My high school classmates and the rest of the country, it seemed, were rebelling by participating in all three of those activities. I was being rebellious too, I guess, by going to see the Cleveland Indians play.

After I was able to drive during my last two years of high school, I spent a lot of time at Municipal Stadium alone in my thoughts watching the Indians play. It was an easy place for a person to be alone with their thoughts. The average attendance for Indians games for 1969 and 1970 was about 8,000. That was in a cavernous stadium which had seen better days, even then, and had over 70,000 seats; 90% of the seats would regularly be empty.

My time spent at baseball stadiums would continue through my lifetime. As much as I can't sit still and am always doing things, being at a baseball game seems to be the one thing I do that keeps me still for a few hours. I can almost feel my blood pressure drop (except when the Indians aren't hitting) when I attend a ball game.

This book is about my life as a baseball fan and starts with a baseball game between the Cleveland Indians and Texas Rangers on a Saturday night in May 2012 at Progressive Field in Cleveland.

CHAPTER ONE

Walk to the Park

I start my trek this Saturday evening, May 5, 2012, to the Indians game. As I leave my apartment, it is 59 degrees outside and I realize that I would need a jacket and went back up to my apartment to get one. It's early May and the warm weather hasn't arrived yet. This summer, though, the hot weather will arrive and it will be one of the hottest summers on record. I started the one mile walk from my apartment to Progressive Field located in the Gateway District of Cleveland.

Progressive Field was built in time for the 1994 baseball season and is a baseball only facility. There was an outdoor college hockey game played there once that I attended. Although it is almost 20 years old, Progressive Field still appears new to me. I'll be one of 494,257 people who will be attending major league baseball games in 15 different venues this evening.

My walk to the ballgame goes along West Huron Road. I have to cross Superior Avenue first. After I cross Superior, on my right on the other side of Huron Road is the twenty-four story Carl B. Stokes Federal Court House.

It appears to have been built out of stainless steel. The building features a flat roof. There is a 37 foot tall bronze statue at the entrance called Cleveland Venus which is a variation on Venus de Milo. The courthouse is named after Carl Stokes who became the first African-American mayor of a major U.S. city when he was elected Cleveland's mayor in 1968. I've been in there to get my license to practice law in Federal Court in Northern Ohio.

As I continue to walk along Huron Road, there is a valley to my right and I can clearly see Cleveland's crooked river, the Cuyahoga. On this particular night, a bulk carrier vessel, the Wicko, with its home port in the Bahamas, is gradually winding its way down the river with the help of a tug boat. It left the Les Escoumins Harbor along the St. Lawrence Seaway in Canada a few days earlier.

The Cuyahoga River is the reason there is a Cleveland. The name, Cuyahoga, is from the Iroquois language and means "crooked river." The original Moses Cleaveland settlement in 1796 was along the Cuyahoga near the mouth of Lake Erie.

At the time he founded the city, Moses was impressed with the land there which was a plain that was full of thick forest. Eighty years after he founded his settlement, there would be a baseball team named after the forest that Moses observed. About a mile from that settlement now is where Progressive Field is located. If Moses were around today, he would be able to see the stadium if he looked uphill from his settlement along the Cuyahoga River. To him it would probably appear to be a large glowing crown.

Moses would be astounded at the city that bore his name that grew out of that humble settlement. If the name of the city looks different from Moses' last name, it is because an "a" was dropped from the name. Different accounts are given for the change from Cleaveland to Cleveland. One is that a newspaper, the Advertiser, could not fit the name Cleaveland on its header without dropping a letter.

Another account is simply a misspelling by a surveyor.

Cleveland was incorporated as a village in 1814 and remained a small town until the Civil War. The war effort brought industry to the city to provide iron, ships, garments and other supplies in support of the North's war effort. After the Civil War, the city would keep growing as different industries continued to move there. The demand for unskilled labor at the factories would also create a migration of workers from throughout the United States, including the southern states, as well as from Europe.

Cleveland would continue to grow and become the sixth largest city in the United States around 1950. It would be a location with a favorable reputation throughout the world as an industrial center. That would change. Soon after 1950, businesses and industries located in Cleveland would begin a long gradual migration to the southern and western parts of the United States as well as to the Far East. The inhabitants of Cleveland would also relocate to the southern and western parts of the United States. Cleveland's population now is less than half of what it was during its heyday.

On this evening, I make this walk to the stadium knowing that I'm embarking on a trip to the ballpark that people here have been taking for over 140 years. The first reference to a major league baseball game in Cleveland is from 1871 and a team called the Forest Citys. The Forest Citys were one of nine teams in the National Association. There was another team in the league that called itself Forest City and it was out of Rockford, Illinois. Modern writers refer to the Cleveland Forest Citys to distinguish it from the Rockford team.

The Forest Citys were provided a new park which was located at Willson and Garden Streets and was near Cleveland's first playground. A season ticket plan was available that year. It went for $6. However, if you wanted to pull up along the first or third baseline in your horse and carriage, then the ticket was $10 for the season.

I'm sure those patrons would be shocked to learn that my ticket for this evening cost $19. On this particular evening, I'm looking forward to seeing favorite Tribe players, Carlos Santana, Asdrubal Cabrera, Shin-Soo Choo and starting pitcher Derek Lowe play ball. I think about how my 1871 counterpart went to the game looking forward to seeing his favorite Forest City players. Their names were Ezra Sutton, Caleb Johnson, Charlie Pabor, also known as "the old woman in the red cap" and young starting pitcher Al Pratt, who would start all 28 games the Forest Citys played that year.

For over the next 140 years, Cleveland baseball fans would travel to the National Association Grounds, League Park, Municipal Stadium and now Progressive Field, formerly known as Jacobs Field, and a few other fields in Cleveland to see professional baseball. Tonight, just as many of those fans did, I would attend the game and I would treat the event with a certain reverence.

One change since then would be the type of fans and their attire. Back in the late 1800s and into the early 1900s almost all baseball fans appear in photographs to be white men dressed up with top hats or bowler hats. I'm sure they would be surprised at the appearance of the fans attending tonight's game.

Tonight's crowd would be much more diverse than the crowd that attended the game back in 1871.

Many of tonight's fans are wearing replica player jerseys and baseball hats. One fact I learned in writing this book is that wearing a baseball hat to show identification with a baseball team did not become popular until Babe Ruth came along years later.

Speaking of uniforms, the Forest Citys wore white shirts with blue trimming, blue hose, a blue belt, russet leather shoes laced tightly to the ankles and a huge monogram of the Cleveland Forest Citys.

Of course, the fans in 1871 would be surprised that I was attending a night baseball game. It would be over 60 years before baseball stadiums would have lights so teams could play baseball at night. The game I will see this evening has also changed a lot from the game in 1871. At the first game in the 1871 season in Cleveland, a single umpire was used and he was chosen from a list provided by the visiting team, the Chicago White Stockings.

The final score in that game was 18-10 and ended in the eighth inning when officers of the Forest City club stopped the game claiming the umpire was too partial to the White Stockings. They claimed that a mistake made by the umpire in the sixth inning allowed the White Stockings to get five "tallies" that they were not entitled to when the umpire missed a call at first base that would have ended the inning.

The fans that afternoon were shouting and hissing at the umpire for his partial rulings favoring the White Stockings. However, the crowd also was shouting and hissing at the home team for their "meekness" in not complaining to the umpire about his decisions.

Some of the Indians would not play tonight due to injuries and that would be similar to the Forest Citys in 1871. A look at an 1871 injury list would include such injuries as chill and fever, badly damaged thumb and inflammatory rheumatism. Today's injury list would include such injuries as a left latissimus dorsi muscle strain, Tommy John surgery and lower back inflammation. (I wonder if that is like rheumatism.)

As I continue my walk to the ballpark, I walk by Cleveland's Terminal Tower on my left. The Terminal Tower was built in the late 1920s and was the fourth tallest building in the world at the time. The building was originally going to be fourteen stories tall but the builders decided to expand the project. Good thing they did as the Tower remains one of Cleveland's most well known landmarks. It also houses Tower City Center which is a mall and the location where Cleveland's commuter rail lines all meet making access to the ballpark, as well as Cleveland's Quicken Loans Arena, easy to Clevelanders who prefer not to drive to these games.

The most prominent business to pedestrians along the Center on West Huron Road is the Hard Rock Cafe. As I walk to the game, the sidewalk is empty except for a middle age couple who are walking from the other direction towards the Hard Rock. Although we were strangers, we said hello to each other.

On this particular evening, the song Graduate by Third Eye Blind played outside the Hard Rock Cafe on its outdoor speakers. Across the street is the 64 foot tall Hard Rock Guitar with neon guitar strings.

As I get closer to Progressive Field, I cross Ontario Street at the beckoning of the traffic officer. Once I get across the street, I am greeted by the ticket scalpers. Ticket scalpers have changed with technology. Many of them use bullhorns to announce what tickets they have and many of them are in contact with other scalpers nearby with their cell phones. Others are on bicycles to cover more territory. The scalpers no longer stand on the block where Progressive Field is located. There was an incident a few years ago where a fight broke out between a couple of scalpers over a popular spot to sell tickets. The police now make them stay off the block.

Who are not outside the stadium this evening are the protesters who appear on Opening Day. The protesters are a group of people who believe that it is racist and inappropriate to use the name Indians, as well as Redskins or Braves, as names of sports teams. They always protest outside of the stadium on the first day of the baseball season. They protest not only the name but the Chief Wahoo logo.

My walk now takes me along the side of the Quicken Loans Arena where the Cavaliers play. As I approach the entrance to Progressive Field, I can hear the voice of Tom Hamilton, the Indians radio announcer, as the pre-game radio show is broadcast on speakers outside the stadium.

After going through a security check, something my 1871 counterparts didn't have to go through, my ticket gets scanned approving my entry into the park. The good news for the Indians is that there is a lineup of fans at the ticket windows which winds about 100 feet towards Ontario Street.

The Indians are giving out Chris Perez replica Indians jerseys to fans this evening. Perez is the Indians closer. Another good sign for the Indians is that they ran out of the free jerseys. That means more people showed up for the game than the Indians expected. The paid attendance for this game will be 21,307.

I have what I refer to as a geek seat. It is a row with a single seat and nestles along the left field line probably within ten feet of the foul line and a few rows in front of the left field wall which is nineteen feet high. I have a twenty-game package which includes all Saturday games. On this evening, I arrived earlier than the fans who regularly sit around me.

Today is Cinco de Mayo and there is Mexican music being played on the stadium speakers and, as always, there are fans below along the railing next to the left field line trying to get autographs from the players. Johnny Damon and Michael Brantley are accommodating them. About this time, the Wahoo Club, which calls itself the official booster club of the Cleveland Indians, is presenting the 2011 Gordon Cobbledick Golden Tomahawk Award to shortstop Asdrubal Cabrera.

Gordon Cobbledick was a sports reporter in Cleveland from 1923 through 1964 except for the time in World War II in which he was a war correspondent. The award is given to the Indians player who has made the most outstanding contribution to the team during the previous season. (It also appears that the award used to be given to the most underrated player on the Indians team. The 1963 award was given to Jerry Kindall who only played in 86 games that year.)

The players start running towards their respective dugouts as the beginning of the game gets closer. Second baseman, Jason Kipnis, lobs a baseball into the stands as he runs toward the dugout. A fan, Tyler Burgess, throws out the ceremonial first pitch.

The Baldwin Wallace Men's Chorus sings the Star Spangled Banner and then they exit the field by walking along the left field line and through the outfield wall. The fans give the singers a round of applause as they walk by and exit.

In 1871, the fans attending the Forest Citys game did not listen to the Star Spangled Banner as it was not performed regularly before baseball games until World War II. As I look around the park at the fans, the scoreboard and the players now taking the field, I notice something new at the stadium this year.

There is a corkscrew like structure on the right field corner roof of the stadium. It holds four wind turbines which look more like steering wheels which are spinning around from the wind. It is providing electricity to the stadium. I also notice the huge American flag located behind the center field wall. It is blowing in towards the field. That leads me to believe that there may not be many home runs tonight and, in fact, there would only be one home run hit. That home run would decide the game.

The game is about to start and a young fan yells "Play Ball." The starting lineups appear on the scoreboard.

Texas Rangers starting lineup

Ian Kinsler	2B
Elvis Andrus	SS
Josh Hamilton	CF
Michael Young	1B
David Murphy	LF
Nelson Cruz	RF
Mike Napoli	C
Mitch Moreland	DH
Alberto Gonzalez	3B

Craig Gentry would pinch hit for Murphy in the 8th inning and then play centerfield

Adrian Beltre would pinch hit for Gonzalez in the 11th inning

Brandon Snyder would replace Gonzalez at 3B in the 11th inning

Starting Pitcher:
Derek Holland would pitch 7 1/3 innings

Relief Pitchers:
Mike Adams would pitch 2/3 of an inning
Alexi Ogando would pitch two innings
Joe Nathan would pitch the last inning

Cleveland Indians starting lineup

Michael Brantley	CF
Jason Kipnis	2B
Asdrubal Cabrera	SS
Carlos Santana	1B
Travis Hafner	DH
Shin-Soo Choo	RF
Shelley Duncan	LF
Jack Hannahan	3B
Lou Marson	C

Johnny Damon will pinch hit for Duncan in the 9th inning and play left field for the rest of the game

Starting Pitcher:
Derek Lowe would pitch six innings

Relief Pitchers:
Nick Hagadone would pitch two innings
Vinnie Pestano would pitch one inning
Joe Smith would pitch the last two innings

CHAPTER TWO

First Inning

The Indians starting pitcher is Derek Lowe who started the game by facing the Texas Rangers leadoff batter, second baseman Ian Kinsler. He worked the count to two balls and no strikes and then Kinsler hit a long fly ball which was caught by left fielder Shelley Duncan.

The Rangers next batter, Elvis Andrus, hit a sharp single into center field. Josh Hamilton came to bat and faced the Indians shift where three infielders position themselves on the right side of the infield. It didn't matter as Hamilton drew a walk putting runners on first and second base.

Michael Young, the Rangers first baseman, then hit a ground ball to second baseman Jason Kipnis. Kipnis, attempting a double play, threw the ball to Asdrubal Cabrera which forced Hamilton out at second base but Cabrera's throw to first was late and Young was safe at first.

David Murphy then drew a walk which loaded the bases. Nelson Cruz hit a ground ball to Asdrubal who threw Cruz out at first. The Rangers did not score in the top of the first.

Pitching for the Rangers was Derek Holland. It raised a question. How many times were there two starting pitchers in a game who were both named Derek? I don't know that answer.

Michael Brantley, the Indians leadoff hitter, struck out swinging. Jason Kipnis grounded out to the second baseman. Asdrubal Cabrera singled sharply to left field but Carlos Santana grounded out to the shortstop who forced Asdrubal at second base which ended the Indians first inning.

Between each of the innings tonight, there is a shot of fireworks. It's not to celebrate anything but to scare the seagulls off the field. Seagulls are probably attracted to Progressive Field as fans discard scraps of food around their seats.

There have been times that the seagulls have created issues at the park. The most notable occasion was on June 11, 2009, when the Indians hosted the Kansas City Royals. The game was tied 3-3 in the bottom of the tenth inning. With runners on first and second and nobody out, Indians batter Shin-Soo Choo hit a soft line drive into center field.

The hit would not have driven home a run except it was hit into an area in shallow center field where there were a dozen seagulls hanging around. The seagulls all took off flying as the ball came at them and after the ball bounced once it appears to have hit a seagull in its wing. The direction of the ball was changed and all the Royals center fielder, Coco Crisp, could do was just watch the ball go by him. A run scored and the Indians won.

That was not the first time that the Indians benefited from critters at Progressive Field. On my birthday, October 5, 2007, the Indians hosted Game Two of the American League Division Series against the New York Yankees.

The Indians won the first game of the best of five series but were down 1-0 in the bottom of the eighth inning. About that time, tiny insects, probably midges, swarmed into Progressive Field. Joba Chamberlain, the Yankees pitcher, appeared to be the target of the midges having a few dozen on his neck throughout the inning. Play was stopped at least once for the Yankees players in the field to be sprayed with bug spray.

Apparently, the bugs were looking for moisture and not food and were attracted to the players' sweat. Chamberlain, who appeared to be distracted by the midges, walked leadoff batter Grady Sizemore. Sizemore would then go to second on a wild pitch. After being bunted over to third base, Sizemore scored on another Chamberlain wild pitch.

The distractions by the midges were credited with disrupting Joba Chamberlain's pitching performance. Joba did not give up a hit that inning. Yankees manager, Joe Torre, later stated that he should have taken his players off the field. I was at that game and there did not appear to be midges in the stands. I also don't recall, except for the time the Yankees were in the field, that the midges were much of a distraction at any other time in the game. The game went into extra innings and the Indians would win in the eleventh inning when Travis Hafner singled home Kenny Lofton for the game winning run.

The next two games of the playoffs were scheduled to be played in Yankee Stadium in New York. The Indians lost Game Three but won Game

Four and moved onto the American League Championship Series against the Boston Red Sox.

Coco Crisp and the Yankees would be involved in another game in Cleveland involving an animal. Coco Crisp was playing center field for the Indians on August 25, 2004. He came to bat for the Tribe in the bottom of the eighth with Casey Blake on third base and two outs. The game was tied 3-3.

The Indians had lost their previous nine games. Also on the field was a squirrel that came onto the field in the third inning and stayed on the field all evening. It never disrupted the game and just hung out on the field all evening. Later, a picture of the Rally Squirrel, as it became to be known, appeared on the scoreboard screen with an Indians jersey superimposed on it.

Crisp put down a drag bunt along the first base line which rolled by the pitcher. By the time Yankees second baseman, Enrique Wilson, reached the ball and threw it to first, Crisp had safely dove into first base and the Tribe took a 4-3 lead which they held onto to win the game. As you might expect, the squirrel received credit for ending the Indians losing streak.

CHAPTER THREE

Second Inning

The second inning started with Rangers catcher, Mike Napoli, hitting a ground ball single off the glove of Derek Lowe. When the next batter, Mike Moreland, grounded out to the first baseman, Napoli went to second base. He went to third base when Alberto Gonzalez bounced out catcher to first baseman. Lowe had already thrown 30 pitches by this time, 18 strikes and 12 balls. He then faced Ian Kinsler for the second time.

Kinsler hit a ground ball towards the third baseman whose throw to first was not in time to get Kinsler out. Napoli scored on the play giving the Rangers a 1-0 lead. Elvis Andrus grounded out to Asdrubal Cabrera to end the inning.

In the Indians half of the second inning, the Tribe did not put up much of a challenge. Travis Hafner hit a fly out to the center fielder. Shin-Soo Choo grounded out shortstop to first and Shelley Duncan popped out to the second baseman.

Now, I have been to many baseball games but the first game I attended was one my Dad took me to in 1959. I wish I could tell you that I remember all this information about the game first hand but all I remember is being there and the score. I went back later to look this information up. It was Sunday,

August 2, 1959, and it was a doubleheader against the Baltimore Orioles.

Fans today probably would find this hard to believe but teams used to play two games in one day and charge only one admission price. Now, I'm not sure what prompted my Dad to take me to this game since his Sunday preference was to take his boat out fishing on Lake Erie and drink beer. On those days that I accompanied him fishing, his one concession to me was that we would listen to the baseball game on the radio.

The Indians had a good team in 1959 and went into that Sunday with a respectable 59-43 record. They would finish second that year 5.0 games behind the American League champion Chicago White Sox. The White Sox would lose the World Series to the Los Angeles Dodgers in six games.

A few players of note played for the Indians that day. The right fielder was one of the most popular and powerful players in the game then, Rocco Domenico "Rocky" Colavito. He hit a home run in the game. Rocky would tie with Harmon Killebrew of the Washington Senators for the American League lead in Home Runs with 42 at the end of the season. Rocky also had 111 RBI's and a .257 batting average that year. Four of those home runs were hit in one game against the Baltimore Orioles.

In what could only be considered a bizarre trade right before the 1960 season, Indians general manager, Frank Lane, would trade Colavito to the

Detroit Tigers for batting average champion, Harvey Kuenn, who was also an outfielder.

The fallout from that 1960 trade was often referred to as the "Curse of Rocky Colavito" as the team would enter into a tailspin that lasted for years afterward. The Indians would not finish second again for 35 years and that would be in 1994 when the season ended with a players' strike.

Harvey Kuenn would play one year with the Indians before he was traded to the San Francisco Giants before the 1961 season. The Indians teams weakened after 1959 and attendance dropped drastically in the 1960s and into the early 1970s.

During those years there was talk of the team relocating to Seattle. Another option that was discussed during that time was the Indians playing some of their home games in New Orleans during the early part of the baseball season.

Prior to the 1965 season, the Indians would trade to get Colavito back. He played for the Kansas City Athletics in 1964. The Indians paid a heavy price to get him back as it was hoped that the trade for him would revive interest in the team. The trade involved three teams. The Indians traded pitcher Tommy John, center fielder Tommie Agee and catcher John Romano to the White Sox who sent players to Kansas City and the Indians received Colavito back.

After the trade, Tommy John would pitch seven seasons for the White Sox and he had a Won-Loss record of 82-80 and a 2.95 ERA for the Sox. Tommy John will always be remembered, though, for an experimental surgical procedure which he would have to extend his pitching career. (The surgery involves taking a tendon from the person being operated on and relocating the tendon around the elbow to strengthen the elbow which, in turn, strengthens the arm.)

The surgery was a success and is common among athletes today. John would win a total of 288 games in his pitching career which spanned 26 years until he retired at the age of 46 in 1989.

Tommie Agee would be the 1966 American League Rookie of the Year while with the White Sox. He would be traded from the White Sox to the New York Mets and be part of the Mets' 1969 World Championship team. Colavito, his best days behind him by the time he returned to Cleveland, had two productive years in Cleveland in 1965 and 1966 but was traded to the White Sox during the 1967 season.

Also playing for the Indians that day in 1959 was Tito Francona who is the father of the 2013 Indians manager, Terry Francona. Tito would go 4 for 4 in the first game and end that game with a .410 batting average. However, his heroics plus the home run by Colavito and another home run by Woodie Held would not be enough for the Indians to win as they lost 5-4 in 10 innings.

I would have liked to stay for the second game but one was plenty for my Dad and we left. Too bad, the Indians would win the second game of the doubleheader 6-3 and Terry's father would go 3 for 4 with a home run and raise his average to .417.

I can't ignore another player on that 1959 Indians team, Jimmy Piersall, who was not in the lineup that day. Piersall played for the Indians for three seasons from 1959 through 1961. Jimmy Piersall's story became a movie "Fear Strikes Out" which portrays his battle with mental illness. Piersall's breakdown is attributed to his father living vicariously through Jimmy's life by pushing him to become a major league baseball player.

Although our names are spelled different, they are pronounced the same and after having studied my genealogy, I can safely conclude that he and I are distant relatives.

I sometimes wonder why I became such a big baseball fan. My Dad would have nothing to do with sports and once told my Mom that he thought ball players must be "queer" to enjoy participating in contact sports with other men.

Another thing that really irritated my Dad was that Jim Brown, the Cleveland Browns superstar running back who was African American, made more money than my Dad did when Brown played in the 1960s.

My Mom was a great piano player but had little interest in sports and I don't think her family did either. However, she was raised in Detroit and she did tell me when the Detroit Tigers won the 1935 World Series how drunk my grandfather got celebrating the World Series victory. She also told me that Tigers catcher, Mickey Cochrane, was my grandfather's favorite baseball player.

(An interesting story here. Not only was Mickey Cochrane my grandfather's favorite baseball player but the favorite baseball player of Elvin Charles "Mutt" Mantle who named his son

"Mickey" after Mickey Cochrane. I remember reading somewhere that Elvin did not realize that Mickey was a nickname. Mickey Cochrane's real name was Gordon Stanley Cochrane.)

As a youngster, I was continually asked about whether I was related to Jimmy Piersall and I probably relished the attention. However, I'm sure the rest of my family got tired of being asked if they were related to him.

Even after I moved to Tampa, I would still get asked if there was a baseball player with my name and whether I was related to him. Now living back in Cleveland, I continue to get that question regularly. I sometimes think that the name similarity made me interested in Piersall's career and the Indians.

I did meet a Pearsall who played professional baseball. In 1996, I attended a Savannah Sand Gnats game in Savannah, Georgia. One of the pitchers that night for the Sand Gnats, a Dodgers' farm club in the South Atlantic League, was J.J. Pearsall. As the game went into extra innings, he came into the stands after he was replaced and I had the opportunity to talk to him briefly. I am sure he and I share distant relatives. J.J. would never pitch in the majors although he did pitch for a couple teams briefly at the AAA level.

As long as I am talking about baseball players named Pearsall, in "Baseball in the Garden of Eden, The Secret History of the Early Game" by John Thorn, there is a reference in the book to a Dr. Andrew Thurstin "Aleck" Pearsall who played both cricket and baseball. He played for the Excelsior Base Ball Club of Brooklyn in the early 1860s.

In 1863, the Excelsior Base Ball Club would expel him from the club as Dr. Pearsall would become a Brigade Surgeon for the Confederacy during the Civil War. It was reported that he continued to play baseball after he joined the Confederacy. After the Civil War, he lived in Montgomery, Alabama and played first base for the Montgomery Base Ball Club. He would move back to Oswego, New York around 1880 and he continued to practice medicine there. He died in Oswego in 1905 at the age of 66.

As I mentioned, one reason I may have become a big baseball fan was the name recognition with Jimmy Piersall. The other reason could be my Dad's drinking habits which conflicted with my Mom's career as a piano teacher. Mom regularly taught piano in our home. She tried to teach me piano but I was not very interested in learning to play. Although I can play the piano a little bit now, I regret not learning to play the piano as my Mom would have desired.

On Saturdays, Mom would teach piano all day in our home and Dad would leave the house while she taught piano. He would usually go to the bar if not out on his boat. Someone had to watch me so it was not unusual for my Dad to take me with him to a bar on North Broadway in Lorain that he referred to as "Hanna's House of Happiness."

There is not much for a child to do in a bar on a Saturday afternoon but watch baseball on the little television up in the corner above the bar. Back in the early 1960s, Saturday baseball games were always played during the day and were televised in glorious black and white as color television was only reserved for Sunday night shows like Bonanza.

Other people at the bar would talk baseball to me. So it probably gave me an opportunity to join in the conversation with my "drinking buddies."

All I was drinking was Pepsi, Coke or sarsaparilla. To this day, I have an aversion to daytime drinking of alcohol because it brings back memories of hanging out at bars when I was a kid.

However I became interested in baseball, it became a big part of my life. Dad would take me to one other baseball game in Cleveland in the 1960s, a Father's Day game which was preceded by a three inning old-timers game of former Indians and All-Stars. I also went to two games with my Mom to see the Indians play. When Dad took me, he would drive.

Mom didn't take me to games as she didn't like driving into Cleveland. If Mom was going to a baseball game with me, I would have to drive. One of the games I took her to was infamous for the gift the Indians gave out. It was Mother's Day in 1971.

The Indians came into Mother's Day with an 8-19 Won Loss record. Only 4,288 people showed up for the game against the California Angels. Due to the small attendance, good seats were available and we sat right behind the third base dugout. As Cleveland Municipal Stadium seated 78,000 for baseball, that meant about 19 of every 20 seats in the stadium were empty. It was so quiet there that when I started yelling encouragement to one of the

Indians, Mom told me to be quiet as she was worried that the player might hear me.

Mom must have been good luck for the Indians as they won that day, 4-1. Alan Foster, the Indians pitcher, pitched a complete game against the Angels. 1971 was the only season he would pitch for the Indians.

Now you might be wondering what the gift was that they gave out to mothers on that Mother's Day. All mothers in attendance that day got a big can of Right Guard deodorant. At least it was the big can. If the Indians played bad enough that day, I guess the mothers in the crowd could spray the field with Right Guard.

It would be 30 years before Mom and I would go to another game. It was a Sunday in April 2001. Again, Mom brought good luck to the Indians as they beat the Texas Rangers 9-2. A lot had changed for the Indians in those 30 years.

There were about ten times as many people at the game in 2001 as there were at the Mother's Day game in 1971 and the only seats we could get were in the upper level in right field. The 2001 Indians would win the division for the sixth time in seven years.

CHAPTER FOUR

Third Inning

The Rangers half of the third inning went quietly. Josh Hamilton grounded out to the third baseman. Michael Young grounded out to the shortstop and David Murphy then struck out.

The Tribe finally got a runner in scoring position in the bottom of the third inning. The first Indians batter that inning was Jack Hannahan. All the players select music to be played before their at bats. Hannahan's was an Irish jig. His song is a contrast to the rock, rap or country music some of the other players have selected to be played before their at bats.

The jig did not help as Jack Hannahan hit a weak ground ball that Rangers shortstop, Elvis Andrus, picked up with his bare hand and threw Hannahan out at first. At this point, Rangers pitcher Derek Holland's pitch count reached 28 pitches, 11 balls and 17 strikes.

Lou Marson then struck out. The Tribe's lead-off hitter, Michael Brantley, doubled down the first base line. When the Indians get a runner in scoring position, John Adams, who has been bringing his bass drum to almost every Indians game since 1973, starts beating his drum.

Tonight was no different as he started the drum beat from his seat in the top row of the bleachers.

Jason Kipnis seemed inspired and hit a sharp grounder but it was right to the first baseman who tagged first base for the third out.

Around this time of the game, I usually take a walk around the park. The way Progressive Field is built, when you walk around the stadium, you lose sight of the field along the third base line as you go underneath the stands. You can see the game on the televisions above the corridor.

More recent stadiums are designed so that no matter where you are, you can see the game as you walk around the stadium. As I walk around to the first base side, I come out from underneath the stands and watch the game while standing behind the seats in the lower level.

I stop and get a hot dog on this trek around the stadium. When you eat a hot dog at an Indians game, you have to use Bertman Ball Park Mustard a/k/a Stadium Mustard. It is a hot spicy mustard and is well known to Cleveland's sports fans. They have been serving it at all sporting events in Cleveland since I've been going to games. What distresses me is that when I go to major or minor league parks elsewhere, many don't carry this mustard.

Some advice about Bertman Mustard. I attended Opening Day on April 6, 2007, when the Indians hosted the Seattle Mariners. The game was continually interrupted by snow. During one of the delays while snow was being blown off the field, I decided to treat myself to a hot dog. I thought it might warm me up.

I bought the hot dog and put the Bertman Mustard on it. I didn't think about the fact that the mustard had been sitting out in the freezing cold weather for a few hours. I was exasperated when I bit into the hot dog and it tasted like it was covered with mustard ice cream.

The mustard is so popular that when I lived in Tampa, Bertman Mustard was the one thing people always asked me to bring them when I returned from Cleveland.

I eat the hot dogs at the Indians games but generally don't drink liquids at the games as I hate to miss part of the game to go to the bathroom. Also, the prices of the drinks at the ballpark are high.

Speaking of other baseball parks, I have been to 89 different parks. It is not unusual to get asked about my favorite baseball park and it is an easy choice. PNC Park in Pittsburgh is my favorite. Living in Cleveland, I can get over there easily and, at least once every baseball season, I make sure to go see the Pirates play. There are many things to like about PNC Park.

One thing I like about PNC, and it is similar to Turner Field and Great American Ballpark in this respect, is that no matter where you are at on the lower level, you can see the playing field. As I mentioned, in most stadiums, you can't see the field as you walk underneath the stands behind the home plate area.

PNC has a beautiful view of the city and I love standing out beyond right field by the Allegheny River and watching the river roll along to meet the Monongahela and create the Ohio River. I have learned that the best seat in PNC is in the upper deck along the third base line where you can see the river while watching the game. It is harder to say what my second favorite stadium is and it is equally hard to say what the worst stadium is that I visited but I have to choose the Metrodome in Minneapolis over Tropicana Field in Tampa or Stade Olympic in Montreal.

The problem I have with the Metrodome is that it is built like an indoor arena. You have to be in your seat to see the game. You can't walk around the stadium and keep an eye on the game as you can with the open air stadiums. Tropicana Field and Stade Olympic are built the same way. The good news is that the Metrodome is no longer used for baseball. Here are some of my favorite stories about stadiums.

As I mentioned, a stadium that I didn't care for was Stade Olympic in Montreal. It was built for the 1976 Olympics and its most prominent feature is the tower that hovers over the stadium which also houses an observatory. I flew to Montreal to see some Expos games after Major League Baseball announced that the Expos would be eliminated along with the Minnesota Twins to reduce the number of baseball teams before the 2002 baseball season.

The reduction was deemed necessary as Major League Baseball did not believe that these two teams could make a profit operating in those cities. Baseball never did go through with this reduction but the Expos franchise would move to Washington, D.C. and become the Washington Nationals starting in the 2005 baseball season. The Twins are still in Minneapolis and have replaced the Metrodome with an outdoor stadium, Target Field.

One of the more entertaining promotions that I have seen at baseball stadiums took place at Stade Olympic. Between one of the innings, I started hearing whistles.

The contest that they were having was for the best dancer. A $50 gift card to a jeans store was the prize. Young women in the crowd were dancing and they blew their whistles to try to get the attention of the camera operator who would put them on the scoreboard screen. The fans would then vote by their applause for the best dancer.

The winning dancer would get an additional $50 added to their gift card if they were wearing jeans from the store that held the contest. It was quite entertaining watching these young women dance to try to win a gift card.

I have seen the Expos franchise play home games in four different stadiums. As I mentioned above, I saw them play at Stade Olympic. As the team continued to struggle with attendance, they decided to play 22 games a season in San Juan.

In 2003, right before I would move from Tampa back to Cleveland, I decided to go to San Juan to see the Expos play games there. The games were held at Hiram Bithorn Stadium. Hiram Bithorn, who was actually Irish, was the first major league player born in Puerto Rico. He played for the Cubs and White Sox in the 1940s. Tragically, he died at the age of 35 when he was shot by a police officer in Mexico in 1951. The police officer who shot him went to prison for eight years for the incident.

Hiram Bithorn Stadium was built in 1962 and its seating capacity was just over 18,000. Due to the limited capacity, tickets for the Expos games were expensive. However, the anticipated big crowds did not show up for the games and I attribute that to the high price of the tickets.

One of the interesting drinks sold by vendors walking through the stands were Pina Coladas. They sold the Pina Coladas until the end of the game. Usually, alcohol sales end before the beginning of the eighth inning at most major league games.

Selling alcohol at the Friday game was going to be an issue since it happened to be Good Friday and alcohol sales were prohibited that day.

It rained so hard on Good Friday that the game was cancelled. I'm not sure the management was upset as they could now sell alcohol at the rescheduled game on Saturday, the first game of a day night doubleheader.

In 2005, after the team moved to Washington, D.C., I went and saw the team play at Robert F. Kennedy Memorial Stadium. RFK, as it was called, was one of the last stadiums that was built for both baseball and football. In 2011, I saw the Nationals play in their new park, Nationals Park.

It was a steamy hot summer day when I visited Nationals Park. It is a new stadium and very spacious. However, driving in the city and parking at the stadium is a frustrating experience at best. The lesson that I should have learned the first time I saw a baseball game in Washington was to use public transportation to get to the game.

Speaking of hot weather, living in Florida as I did until 2003, I saw a many games in the heat. A friend of mine and I went to see the Florida Marlins play in Miami during their first season in 1993. It was so hot that my friend was unable to sit out in the sun. He ended up watching the game from underneath the stands in the shade.

I attended games during summers in Atlanta on steamy hot days and I remember one day it was so hot that I thought I saw a fan passed out in the stands.

Years ago I traveled to Texas to see games in Arlington and Houston. I spent a Saturday night in Houston and walked over to the Astrodome from my hotel across the street. The game was a 6 o'clock start.

I purposely stayed at that hotel to save on the cost of parking at the stadium.

When I walked from the hotel to the stadium, it was so hot and muggy that I had to walk back to the hotel, take a shower and drive my car across the street and park as close to the entrance as I could so I wouldn't be soaked with sweat before I went into the park. Once I got into the Astrodome, though, I froze. I swear the air conditioning was set at 70 degrees. The next day, I stopped at a mall in Houston to get another shirt since I was out of clean shirts.

I drove back to Arlington for a 6:05 p.m. Sunday game. The reason the game was at 6:05 instead of earlier in the afternoon was due to the hot weather. It didn't matter; it was 102 degrees at game time. Everybody in the stands where I was sitting knew I was wearing a new shirt since I forgot to remove the tag.

CHAPTER FIVE

Fourth Inning

In the fourth inning, the Rangers first batter, Nelson Cruz, grounded a single into center field. Mike Napoli did exactly the same and Cruz stopped at second base. The Rangers designated hitter, Mike Moreland, then doubled off the right field wall. Cruz scored and the Rangers had runners on second base and third base with still nobody out.

In a strange play, Alberto Gonzalez hit a sharp grounder to shortstop Asdrubal Cabrera who tagged Moreland who was off second base. Asdrubal threw to first base to get the double play. Mike Napoli didn't try to score from third base. Ian Kinsler came to bat with two outs and grounded out to the Indians third baseman, Jack Hannahan, to end the inning. The Rangers now had a two run lead.

In the Indians half of the fourth inning, Cabrera grounded out to the first baseman and Carlos Santana then struck out. Travis Hafner drew a walk. Shin-Soo Choo worked a two ball no strike count. That drew a visit from the Rangers pitching coach, Mike Maddux, to the mound to talk to Holland. On the next pitch after that visit, Choo would fly out to the left fielder for the third out.

As I mentioned in the previous chapter, I walk around the stadium during the game. There is a sign which marks the location of a future Jim Thome statue. Outside the stadium near the center field entrance is a statue of Bob Feller.

Bob Feller is probably the most iconic Cleveland Indians player having pitched for the Indians starting in 1936 after he signed a contract for $1 and a baseball as his bonus. He pitched for the Indians through 1956. Bob Feller's pitching statistics are legendary.

Like so many of his generation, "Rapid Robert" as he was known, volunteered to fight in World War II. Over three years of his baseball life were lost due to military service.

After his baseball career was over, he stayed in great shape, often throwing out the first pitch at the Indians opener. He was 92 when he passed away in 2010. He still lived in the area all these years after he stopped playing and I think everyone in the Cleveland area has at least one Bob Feller autographed baseball.

During those years after World War II, the Indians had a great baseball team, regularly challenging for the American League title and winning it in 1948 and 1954. They won the World Series in 1948 over the Boston Braves. That was the last Indians team to win the World Series. In many ways, his statue is homage to that era's Cleveland Indians.

Similarly, Jim Thome played for the Indians from 1991 to 2002. From 1995 through 2001, the Indians won their division and went to the playoffs six times, appearing in two World Series. In many ways, his statue pays homage to those teams. At the time of this writing, Jim Thome is no longer playing but he did return to the Indians during 2011 to help in their push to a playoff spot that, unfortunately, they didn't reach. Thome is still hopeful of getting an opportunity to play again.

However, there is no Sam Jethroe statue and probably no talk of one. So Cleveland fans may wonder why I talk about a statue for Sam Jethroe. To most baseball fans, Sam played in the major leagues for the Boston Braves from 1950 though 1952 and was National League Rookie of the Year in 1950. He was 33 in his rookie season. He played in 1953 for the Toledo Sox in the American Association and was traded to Pittsburgh in 1954 but played just two games for the Pirates.

Afterward, he played five seasons for the Toronto Maple Leafs, a minor league baseball team in the International Association. During his major league career, he played all three outfield positions, had a batting average of .261, hit 49 home runs, drove in 181 runs and stole 98 bases. He led the National League in stolen bases twice in his short major league career.

Cleveland fans saw him play, though, and saw him at his greatest. The fans remember how in 1945, he led his Cleveland major league baseball team in the American League to a World Championship beating a Pittsburgh team from the National League in the World Series. It happened. It really did.

Physics professors and philosophers refer to a parallel universe as a hypothetical self-contained reality coexisting with one's own. In Cleveland in the 1940s it was not a hypothetical. While the Cleveland Indians played in an all white major league, the Cleveland Buckeyes played in an all black major league. The fans who saw Sam Jethroe play and saw the Buckeyes win the Negro League World Series in 1945 were predominantly African-American.

From 1926 through the late 1930s, most black baseball teams in Cleveland lasted just about a season or more before going out of business.

In 1941, a hotel and nightclub owner from Erie, Pennsylvania, Ernest Wright, organized the Cleveland Buckeyes who were to play in the Negro American League. In 1942, the team was known as the Cleveland-Cincinnati Buckeyes but made their home permanently in Cleveland from 1943 through 1948.

As black Clevelanders prospered from the work necessary to build supplies demanded by the Second World War, the Buckeyes allowed black Clevelanders a place to congregate and spend their money.   Cleveland was a segregated city like many other cities of its time. As the major league teams had yet to integrate, black baseball provided a sense of pride and community to black Clevelanders.

Many people don't understand how Negro League baseball operated. It was a cross between the Harlem Globetrotters and organized baseball.

During the years the Buckeyes were in existence, there was no television. If a person wanted to see a baseball game, he or she would have to attend one. During the week, the Buckeyes would travel around to cities from Dayton, Ohio to Syracuse, New York and cities in between and play games against local teams, many of them consisting of all white players.

On weekends and holidays, the black teams would play organized league games against other teams in the Negro League. Each season had a first half winner and a second half winner. If different teams won the first and second half, they would have a playoff series. Many of those playoff games would be played in neutral sites. At the end of every season, there was a World Series between the winners of the Negro American League and the Negro National League.

Many of these Cleveland Buckeye players, including Sam Jethroe, never really got their proper recognition as major league professional baseball players.

Jethroe was referred to as Sammy by Cleveland's black newspaper, the Call and Post. Like many African Americans at the time, there are different reports of his place and date of birth. He played center field for the Buckeyes each year of their existence from 1942 through 1948.

Jethroe was talented enough that the Boston Red Sox brought him, Jackie Robinson and Marvin Williams, an infielder for the Negro League Philadelphia Stars, to Boston for a tryout in 1945. However, the event was more of a showcase to appease local politicians who were threatening to take away the Red Sox permit to play baseball on Sunday as pressure to integrate major league baseball after World War II started to increase.

At that "tryout" in Boston, high school pitchers were brought in to pitch to the players. The three players never heard from the Red Sox management afterward. It should be noted too that the last Major League team to integrate was the Red Sox. That occurred when Jerry "Pumpsie" Green was promoted to their roster in July 1959.

As mentioned above, Jethroe did have some success in the major leagues, but the peak of his baseball skills occurred while he was playing for the Buckeyes. Their most memorable season was 1945.

The 1945 Buckeyes were led by catcher and manager, Quincey Trouppe. He was born Quincey Troupe on Christmas Day in 1912 in Dublin, Georgia. His father, Charles Troupe, later moved his family to St. Louis to get away from the deep segregated south. Quincey was an excellent athlete and played professional baseball for a time in Mexico where his team added an additional "p" to his last name making it Trouppe, pronounced Troup-pe'. He liked the sound of the name and kept the spelling and pronunciation.

Quincey would make it to the Major Leagues playing for the Cleveland Indians in 1952. However, he only played in six games for the Tribe that year. Many of the pitchers were reluctant to pitch to a black catcher. Quincey then played the remainder of that year for the Indianapolis Indians of the American Association. He finished his professional career in Mexico.

Besides being an intelligent ballplayer, Quincey was an excellent scout and would eventually become a scout for the St. Louis

Cardinals. His scouting skills were in fine form before the 1945 Buckeyes season as he would sign Avelino Canizares to play shortstop for the Buckeyes.

Avelino was born in Cuba and played primarily in Mexico. The only year he played in the Negro Leagues was 1945. He was one of many great Hispanic baseball players that also don't get their due as they didn't play in the white Major Leagues like other Hispanic ballplayers did.

Sam Jethroe was definitely the star of the 1945 team. He would lead the Negro Leagues in batting with an average over .400 late into August 1945. He also led the Negro Leagues in triples and stolen bases. Jackie Robinson, by comparison, was batting .340 at the same time.

The 1945 Buckeyes lineup would look like this: Avelino Canizares SS, Archie Ware 1B, Sammy Jethroe CF, Parnell Woods 3B, Willie Grace RF, Quincey Trouppe C, Buddy Armour LF and Johnny Cowan 3B. The pitcher would bat last in the lineup. The pitching staff that year included Gene Bremer, Frank Carswell and brothers Willie Jefferson and George Jefferson.

In 1945, the Cleveland Buckeyes won both the first and second half of the Negro American League season and met the Negro National League champion, Homestead Grays, in the World Series. The Homestead Grays called Pittsburgh their home.

The first two World Series games were scheduled to be played in Cleveland. Those games were scheduled three days apart as the Buckeyes and Grays scheduled an exhibition game between those dates in Dayton. The Buckeyes also played an exhibition game between the end of the regular season and before the World Series against the Chattanooga Choo Choos of the Negro Southern League.

Game Three of the World Series was scheduled to be played in Pittsburgh and Game Four of the World Series was scheduled to be played in Washington, D.C. The Homestead Grays, although calling Pittsburgh their home, played many of their games in Washington. If Games Five and Six of the World Series were necessary, they would be played in Philadelphia and New York City, respectively. Game Seven, if necessary, would be played back in Cleveland.

The Homestead Grays were appearing in their fourth straight World Series and featured such Negro League legends as Cool Papa Bell, Josh Gibson and Buck Leonard.

Cool Papa Bell played left field. He played 21 seasons in the Negro Leagues and his career average is reported to be .316.

Josh Gibson was the Grays catcher. Many baseball historians refer to Josh Gibson as the black "Babe Ruth" and state that he may have hit as many as 800 home runs in his career. However, he died tragically young at 35 and many people believe it was from drug problems.

Buck Leonard played first base for the Grays. Leonard played 15 seasons in the Negro Leagues and his lifetime average was .320. He came into the 1945 World Series with a .281 regular season average. The Grays were heavily favored to win the World Series.

The first game of the World Series was played on September 13, 1945. 6,500 fans showed up at League Park in Cleveland. Willie Jefferson pitched for the Buckeyes and Roy Welmaker pitched for the Grays. Neither team scored until the bottom of the seventh inning when Quincey Trouppe tripled and scored on Johnny Cowans' sacrifice fly. The Buckeyes scored a second run in the eighth inning when Archie Ware scored on Willie Grace's single. They led 2-0 going into the top of the ninth inning. Josh Gibson singled for the Grays with one out but the game ended when the Grays shortstop, Sam Bankhead, grounded into a double play.

The Grays would win the exhibition game against the Buckeyes in Dayton on the next day. On Sunday, September 16, a cool day in Cleveland, 10,000 fans showed up for Game Two of the series. The Grays led the game 2-0 going into the bottom of the seventh inning. Willie Grace, who was also known as the "St. Louis Slugger," would lead off the inning with a home run over the Gem Safety Razor ad in right field. As he crossed the plate, Buckeyes fans showered him with money as was the custom. His home run was the only home run hit by either team in the World Series.

Buddy Armour would then double and score when Buckeyes pitcher, Eugene Bremer, hit a ground ball that was muffed by Jelly Jackson, the Grays second baseman. Armour scored from second as the ball rolled into right field. The score was tied

2-2. Bremer kept the Grays from scoring in the eighth and ninth inning.

Leading off the bottom of the ninth, Trouppe led off with a double. He went to third base on a wild pitch. The Grays walked the next two Buckeye batters, Armour and Cowan, to load the bases and set up a force at every base. The next batter was again Buckeyes pitcher, Eugene Bremer. The fans groaned when he was left into bat for himself instead of a pinch hitter. However, he hit a ground rule double to right field which scored Trouppe and the Buckeyes took the series lead two games to none.

Newspapers reported the final score to be 4-2 as Bremer was credited with a double. However, baseball statisticians list the final score as 3-2 stating that Bremer should only have received credit for a single since that is the only number of bases he needed to score the winning run and is credited with only one run batted in.

The pitcher for the Grays in Game Two was John Wright. His name has been lost in history but Wright was the second African-American player signed by Organized Baseball and reported to spring training with the Brooklyn Dodgers in 1946 along with Jackie Robinson.

He was one of the people to greet Jackie Robinson when Jackie arrived for spring training in Daytona Beach by Greyhound bus. However, Wright would not make the major leagues and would be back playing for the Homestead Grays in 1947.

The third game was scheduled to be played in Pittsburgh but was rained out. It was not to be made up there and the series continued to the venue that was scheduled for Game Four of the series, Griffith Stadium in Washington, D.C.

6,000 people showed up on September 18 on a rainy night. As the train was running late, the Buckeyes had to go straight from the train station to play the game and got there just as the Detroit Tigers and Washington Senators were completing an afternoon game.

Grays fans would be disappointed again as the Buckeyes' George Jefferson, Willie's brother, pitched a complete game shutout as the Buckeyes won 4-0. Avelino Canizares' excellent fielding was a paramount reason the Buckeyes were able to shutout the Grays in the game.

Game Four of the World Series was played at Shibe Park in Philadelphia. That game was no contest as the Buckeyes' Frank Carswell shutout the Grays who only managed four hits off of him. On one play in Game Four, Sammy Jethroe made a great catch but was injured running into the center field wall. Buckeyes General Manager, Dr. Wilbur Hayes, sprinted out to administer medical assistance to Jethroe but part of the way out developed a charley horse and needed medical assistance himself. The Buckeyes scored five runs on ten hits against Grays pitcher, Ray Brown. It was reported that the Philadelphia fans would not return foul balls hit into the crowd.

Only four Cleveland pitchers were used in the series as they all pitched complete games. The attendance for the four games was 35,000. Quincey Trouppe led all batters with a .400 batting average and a .600 slugging percentage. The Buckeyes brought the World Championship back with them to Cleveland. The Buckeyes would attend a dinner in their honor at the Rose Room at the Hotel Majestic. The 1945 season would be their only championship season. They finished in fourth place in 1946.

That 1946 team is notable for the fact that the Buckeyes became the only Negro League team to sign a white ballplayer, Eddie Klep. He was released after three pitching appearances.

In Birmingham, Alabama in 1946, the local authorities would not allow the Buckeyes to use Klep in a game as the law prohibited blacks and whites from playing baseball on the same field at the same time.

In 1947, the Buckeyes still had many of the same players as the 1945 Buckeyes including Sammy Jethroe. They went on to win the American Negro League and play the New York Cubans in the World Series. However, they would lose that series four games to one with one game tied. 1947 was the last season of note for the Buckeyes and the Negro Leagues. With Robinson and Wright being signed by the Dodgers and the Indians signing of Larry Doby, the first African American to play in the American League, interest in the Negro Leagues began to wane.

The Cleveland Call and Post, the newspaper for the African-American community in Cleveland, would concentrate more on Larry Doby's career with the Indians than the Buckeyes team. Sammy Jethroe's best years would be forgotten and there is no Sammy Jethroe statue or talk of one.

CHAPTER SIX

Fifth Inning

The Rangers threatened to score again in the top of the fifth inning. Elvis Andrus singled into right field and Josh Hamilton followed with a single of his own putting runners on first and second with no outs. Michael Young hit a ground ball to Asdrubal Cabrera who tagged second base and threw to first for the double play. Andrus advanced to third base.

This was one of the Indians plans in 2012, to strengthen their infield defense and have the pitcher pitch to contact. Instead of striking batters out, which can wear out a pitcher's arm, a pitch is made with the hope that the hitter will hit a ground ball to an infielder. It was a successful strategy this inning.

Dale Murphy then struck out leaving Andrus stranded at third base. (So much for pitching to contact)

In the Indians half of the fifth inning, Shelley Duncan led off the inning and struck out. Jack Hannahan then drew a walk only to have Lou Marson ground out to Rangers shortstop Elvis Andrus who tagged second and threw to first for the double play. Other team's pitchers pitch to contact too.

As I mentioned earlier, many fans wear replica team jerseys when they attend Indians games. I have many of the Indians replica jerseys. One reason teams use different uniforms and accompanying hats is to sell more products. I wear the jersey and hat that matches the one the Indians are wearing for that game.

Weekend home games feature their cream color jerseys with the word "INDIANS" in red block letters across the chest. I don't have a number on the back of my jersey as some people do. These cream color jerseys the players wear do not have their names on their back as the other Indians jerseys do.

One of the fans in the section that I sit in wears the replica Indians jersey from the 1920 season which is the first season the Indians won the World Series. This jersey has a black armband. The armband was worn on the Indians jersey late in the 1920 season after the death of Ray Chapman. His was one of two Cleveland players deaths in the early 1900s which would foreshadow future events in baseball.

Ray Chapman played shortstop for the Cleveland Indians from 1912 into the 1920 season. A right handed batter, he came to bat against New York Yankees right handed pitcher, Carl Mays, in the fifth inning of a game at the Polo Grounds on August 16, 1920. Mays regularly pitched the baseball with an underhand motion and had a reputation for throwing the ball inside to batters to chase them off the plate.

The count was one ball and one strike on Chapman when Mays threw a pitch that would hit Chapman. Baseball players at the time did not wear batting helmets. Helmets would not appear in a major league baseball game until 1937 when the Indians and the Philadelphia Athletics would experiment with them during a game.

The Pittsburgh Pirates in 1953 were the first team to require their players to wear helmets. Those helmets appeared on the 1955 Topps baseball cards that featured Pirates players. Major League Baseball did not require all batters to wear helmets until 1971.

Before Chapman was hit by the pitched baseball, one baseball would last about 100 pitches. If a baseball went into the stands, the fans were prompted to throw the ball back so it could continue to be used. It was not unusual for a baseball to become unraveled, softened up and lopsided during the game. Also, pitchers were allowed to scuff the ball, spit on it, often with tobacco juice, and do other things to the ball to give the pitchers an advantage.

Mays also threw the spitball. On this particular day, it was rainy and the ball was naturally damp.

The pitch struck Ray Chapman in his left temple. Chapman's skull was fractured and his nerve chords were paralyzed making him unable to talk. Chapman would die the next day becoming the only major league player to die from a pitched baseball. After his passing, Major League Baseball required umpires to change baseballs when they got dirty. Now baseballs last about six pitches and there are about 46 used during a baseball game. Ray Chapman joined another Cleveland baseball player who died during his baseball playing days.

On Friday, October 2, 1908, the Cleveland Naps hosted the Chicago White Sox at League Park in Cleveland. The Naps, White Sox and Detroit Tigers were in a three way race for first place with just a few days left in the season. There were 10,598 fans at the game to see Addie Joss pitch for the Naps against Ed Walsh of the White Sox.

Three days before this game, Ed Walsh pitched both games of a doubleheader and won both games for the White Sox.

A note here about the name Naps. Unlike today, baseball teams did not have regular names. Often, their names came from references in local papers. Nap Lajoie was a player manager for the Cleveland team and the papers referred to the team as the Naps. Eventually, baseball would start to name their teams and protect those names by trademark. The name Indians would not become the official name of the team until 1915. Before Nap Lajoie was acquired by the Cleveland baseball team, they were know as the Bronchos. That was the name of the team in 1902 when Addie Joss signed with them.

In the October 2 game against the White Sox, Addie Joss allowed no White Sox player to reach base and it was the second perfect game in the history of the American League. However, the Naps would finish the season in second place, one half game behind the Detroit Tigers. That would be the closest Joss would come to being in a World Series. However, he would be the reason for the first All Star Game.

Joss pitched two more years for the Naps and, through 1910, his career record was impressive to say the least. He had a 1.89 career Earned Run Average, second best in the history of baseball to Ed Walsh. He won 160 games through 1910 and 45 of those games were shutouts.

On April 3, 1911, towards the end of spring training, the Naps played an exhibition game in Chattanooga, Tennessee. Joss was pitching and collapsed from heat prostration. He was taken to a hospital. After being released from the hospital, he traveled with the team to Toledo where, on April 10, the Naps played an exhibition game.

Toledo was Joss' hometown and he went to see his family doctor. He was diagnosed with pleurisy and was told not to play for at least a month. Pleurisy is inflammation of the lining around the lungs. During this time, Joss had been coughing regularly, had severe headaches, could not stand on his own and had slurred speech. A second opinion from the team doctor on April 13 was the diagnosis of tuberculosis meningitis, commonly referred to as TB. The disease had spread to Joss' brain and on April 14, he died. He was 31.

His funeral was scheduled for April 17 which was the same day as the Detroit Tigers season opener in which they were hosting the Naps. The owners of the team decided the game would be played. That meant Joss' teammates would not be able to attend the funeral. The players signed a petition and presented it to Naps management stating that they were going to attend the funeral and not play the game. The players attended the funeral and the game in Detroit had to be rescheduled. Headlines reported "Cleveland Players Strike" but it didn't matter to the players.

The Naps' players decided to have a fundraiser to benefit Joss' family. They came up with an idea for an All Star Game and invited some of the best players in the American League to Cleveland on July 24 of that year for the game.

Five other American League teams did not have scheduled games that day so the best players of those teams came to Cleveland for the benefit game. It was not approved by the American League management but the players appeared anyway along with over 15,000 fans. The American League All Star team played the Naps in a game the All Stars won 5-3.

The first major league baseball All Star Game was a success. Over $12,000.00 was raised to help Addie Joss' family pay remaining medical bills. It would be twenty years later, but Major League Baseball would schedule an All Star Game, sometimes two a season, and the All Star Game has been part of the baseball season at all levels since then.

An interesting note about the 1911 game. Ty Cobb's trunk was lost along with his Detroit Tigers uniform. He can be seen in the official All Star team photo wearing a Cleveland uniform that he had to borrow for the game.

CHAPTER SEVEN

Sixth Inning

The Rangers sixth inning started when Nelson Cruz grounded out to the shortstop and then Mike Napoli grounded out to the second baseman. Mike Moreland, after a 2-2 count, hit a ground ball to Asdrubal Cabrera whose throw pulled Carlos Santana off of first base. It was ruled a hit. Alberto Gonzalez then grounded out to Santana at first and the Rangers minimal threat ended.

The Tribe started a two out rally in the bottom of the sixth inning. After Brantley grounded out to the third baseman, Alberto Gonzalez, and Kipnis hit a hard line drive that Gonzalez also snagged, Asdrubal singled into left field and Santana drew a walk. However, nothing would come of this rally as Travis Hafner hit a soft ground ball to the first baseman for the final out.

I have been to six World Series games and four of those were sixth games so the sixth inning is a good segue to the baseball story of my life.

It's August 1986. My niece Nancy was starting her senior year at Boston University. She had started college in Atlanta at Emory University where I had visited her at least once and decided to visit her again in her senior year now while she was in school in Boston. A better idea came to mind. I thought; why not treat her to a weekend in New York City as a graduation gift. I checked airline and hotel prices, contacted Nancy, and we came up with a plan for her to spend a weekend with me in the Big Apple. We both would arrive on Friday, October 23 and spend a couple of quality days together. That's the kind of uncle that I am, or so I thought.

I had been to New York City in 1983 over the 4th of July weekend and saw Dave Righetti's no-hitter and had a great time during that long holiday weekend. I love going to New York City and thought this would be a great opportunity to revisit the city.

At the time I made the flight and hotel reservations in August, the Boston Red Sox had a four game lead over the New York Yankees in the American League Eastern Division and the California Angels had a two and a half game lead over the Texas Rangers in the American League Western Division.

In the National League, the New York Mets had a 16 game lead over the Montreal Expos and the Houston Astros had a five game lead over the San Francisco Giants in their respective division races.

I was, of course, following the pennant race but since October baseball was still a ways off, I didn't give much thought to any possible baseball conflict with this trip. It so happened that the weekend of the trip to New York City would coincide with the scheduled games six and seven of the World Series.

The 1986 regular season division races were anticlimactic, especially in the National League where the Mets won the Eastern Division by 21.5 games over the second place Philadelphia Phillies. The Astros won the Western Division by 10 games over the second place Cincinnati Reds. In the American League, the Red Sox came in first place, 5.5 games over the second place Yankees. My Indians came in fifth in the Division with a respectable, for them, 84-78 record. The California Angels finished five games ahead of the Rangers for the Western Division championship.

As unexciting as the regular seasons races were, the 1986 post-season would be especially memorable. Tragically, within three years of that post-season, one of the major actors would take his own life. The National League Championship Series featured the two teams from the 1962 National League expansion, the Mets and the Astros. The first two games of the best of seven series were played in Houston. In Game One, the Astros starting pitcher, Mike Scott, pitched a shutout and the Astros won the game 1-0 on a second inning home run by Glenn Davis. In Game Two, the Astros Nolan Ryan was the losing pitcher and the Mets won 5-1.

The series shifted to New York for three games. In Game Three, the Mets were down 5-4 going into the bottom of the ninth inning. With one out and a runner on second base, Lenny Dykstra, the Mets center fielder, hit a two run home run to win the game giving the Mets a two game to one series lead. Mike Scott, pitching on three days rest, was the winning pitcher in Game Four as the Astros won the game 3-1. The series was tied at two games each.

Game Five would be another pitching duel featuring starting pitchers Nolan Ryan for the Astros and Dwight Gooden for the Mets. Each team only scored once through eleven innings. Gary Carter's one out single, in the bottom of the twelfth inning, would drive in the winning run to give the Mets a 3-2 series lead. The series would then return to Houston.

Game Six in Houston would turn out to be a classic playoff game and could have easily been the most memorable post-season game in 1986 except for the game I would later attend. Bob Knepper was the starting pitcher for the Astros and shut the Mets out through eight innings as the Astros took a 3-0 lead going into the top of the ninth inning. However, the Mets had another come from behind rally that would be their trademark during this post-season. They scored three runs in the top of the ninth inning to tie the game which would remain tied through 13 innings. In the top of the fourteenth inning, Wally Backman would single home Darryl Strawberry for a 4-3 Mets lead.

In the bottom of the fourteenth inning, the Astros' Billy Hatcher would hit a home run to tie the game. Neither team would score in the fifteenth inning. Three runs in the sixteenth for the Mets gave them a 7-4 lead. Jesse Orosco, the Mets relief pitcher who came in to pitch in the bottom of the fourteenth inning, had the opportunity to win the game and series for the Mets. With one out, he gave up a walk and two singles and the Astros would trim the Mets lead to 7-6.

With runners on first and second and two outs, the Astros right fielder, Kevin Bass, would strike out to end the game. The next stop for the Mets was the World Series. If the World Series were to go to six games, I would have a dilemma when Nancy and I visited New York City.

The American League Championship Series would be just as exciting. The best of seven series would start at Fenway Park in Boston and the California Angels would win Game One easily after getting seven runs off of Red Sox starter Roger Clemens in 7 1/3 innings. The final score was 8-1. Game Two was also a rout as the Red Sox beat the Angels 9-2, scoring three runs each in both the seventh and eighth innings. The series moved to Anaheim for three games.

Game Three was won by the Angels 5-3. Home runs hit by the Angels' Dick Schofield and Gary Pettis in the seventh inning gave the Angels a 4-1 lead. However, Donnie Moore, the Angels closer, in a prophetic appearance, would give up two runs in the top of the eighth inning to make the game close. The Angels held on to win and had a 2-1 lead in the series.

Game Four was also won by the Angels. They needed some last minute heroics to win the game. Going into the bottom of the ninth inning down 3-0, Doug DeCinces hit a lead off home run against Roger Clemens. After George Hendrick grounded out, Dick Schofield and Bob Boone each had singles. Calvin Schiraldi was then brought in to relieve Clemens and gave up a double to Gary Pettis which scored Schofield.

After an intentional walk to Ruppert Jones which loaded the bases, Schiraldi struck out Bobby Grich. Brian Downing then got hit by a pitch driving in the tying run. After Reggie Jackson grounded out, the game went into extra innings.

Neither team scored in the tenth and after the Red Sox failed to score in the top of the eleventh, Jerry Narron singled to lead off the bottom of the eleventh and moved to second base on a sacrifice. After another intentional walk to Ruppert Jones, Bobby Grich singled home Narron and the Angels won the game and had a 3-1 series lead over the Red Sox.

In Game Five, it appeared the Angels were ready to wrap up the series. Going into the top of the ninth they led the Red Sox 5-2. The Angels starter, Mike Witt, was still in the game and gave up a lead off single to Bill Buckner. After striking out Jim Rice, a former Angel, Don Baylor, came to bat. Baylor played for the Angels for six years and was signed by the Red Sox before the 1986 season. He was primarily a designated hitter and did what they signed him for when he hit a home run to tighten the score at 5-4.

After Dwight Evans made the second out by popping out, Gary Lucas was brought in to relieve Mike Witt and hit Rich Gedman with a pitch. Donnie Moore was brought in to relieve Lucas. Moore then gave up a home run to Dave Henderson and the Angels found themselves down a run going into the bottom of the ninth inning.

The Angels would manage to tie the game up in the bottom of the ninth to send the game into extra innings. Neither team scored in the tenth and Donnie Moore was still pitching when the Red Sox came to bat in the top of the eleventh. Moore hit the first batter, Don Baylor, and then gave up singles to Dwight Evans and Rich Gedman. Dave Henderson then hit a sacrifice fly to score Don Baylor for their only run in the inning. It gave the Red Sox a 7-6 lead going into the bottom of the eleventh.

The first two Angels batters in the bottom of the eleventh, Wilfong and Schofield, struck out and Brian Downing hit a foul pop out to end the inning and the series went back to Boston with the Angels up 3 games to 2. Game Six in Boston was a Red Sox rout as Angels starter Kirk McCaskill gave up seven Red Sox runs in 2 1/3 innings. The series was tied 3-3 going into a dramatic Game Seven.

Game Seven turned out, though, to be anything but dramatic as the Red Sox had a 7-0 lead after four innings. Red Sox starter Roger Clemens only gave up one run to the Angels in seven innings and the Red Sox easily went on to win the game and the series.

The home run that Donnie Moore gave up in Game Five was on a 2-2 count to Dave Henderson. The Angels had never been to the World Series and were one strike away from the World Series when Henderson hit his home run.

Donnie Moore had pitched in the major leagues since 1975 and was primarily a relief pitcher having started just four games during his career. He became a closer in 1984 and had 16 saves for the Braves that year. After joining the Angels in 1985, he had 31 saves that year and 21 saves in 1986.

After giving up that home run in Game Five, Moore would always be associated with the Angels loss of the pennant that year. They Angels were an expansion team in 1961 and had never appeared in a World Series. It would be 16 more years before they would finally make it to the World Series. When Donnie Moore appeared in games for the Angels in 1987 and 1988, the fans would boo him, sometimes mercilessly, as he came on the field. He was released by the Angels after the 1988 season.

As I mentioned, it would be 16 years before the Angels would get to the World Series, making their only appearance in 2002. They would win the World Series that year in seven games beating the San Francisco Giants. Donnie Moore would not be around to see that Series.

In 1989, Donnie Moore would sign with the Kansas City Royals but did not make the major league roster out of spring training. He would pitch for the Omaha Royals, their AAA minor league team in the American Association. He appeared in seven games for Omaha and had a 6.39 earned run average when he was released.

On July 18, 1989, Moore and his wife, Tonya, were having an argument in their Anaheim Hills home. Moore would shoot her three times. After his daughter drove her to the hospital, Donnie Moore would commit suicide by shooting himself at his home while one of his sons was around. Tonya would survive the shooting.

Back to the World Series, the participants had been set. It would be the Red Sox and the Mets and the first two games and the last two games, if necessary, would be played in New York City. The New York Mets had appeared in two World Series before this one, in 1969 and 1973.

The 1969 Mets were known as the Amazin' Mets. Back in 1962, the Mets were an expansion team and never had a winning record until the 1969 season. They were the first expansion team to appear in a World Series. The 1969 season was also the first time the American and National Leagues were separated into two divisions and a team had to win a playoff series to get to the World Series.

In the playoffs, the Mets swept the Atlanta Braves in three games to get to the World Series where they beat the Baltimore Orioles in five games. In 1973, the Mets won the best of five series against the Cincinnati Reds to meet the Oakland A's in the World Series. The Mets would have a 3-2 game lead in the World Series that year when it went back to Oakland for the last two games. However, the A's pitching would hold the Mets batters in check and win games six and seven by scores of 3-1 and 5-2. Before 1986, these would be the Mets only World Series appearances.

The Red Sox had a much different World Series history. The franchise would appear in the World Series five times from 1903 through 1918. They won the first World Series ever in 1903 when they were known as the Boston Americans. They would win all five World Series appearances that they made during those years.

They would also win the American League championship in 1904 but John McGraw, the manager of the National League champion New York Giants, decided his team would not participate in a World Series as he believed the American League was a much inferior league to the National League. His attitude was that his Giants were the Major League champion.

After the 1919 season, the Red Sox would sell one of their most successful pitchers, who also could handle the bat, Babe Ruth, to the New York Yankees. The trade was made so that the Red Sox owner could finance a Broadway play. During the next 66 seasons, the Boston Red Sox would win only three American League championships.

This drought was often blamed on the sale of Ruth and is referred to as "The Curse of the Bambino" which was the superstition that was used to explain the Red Sox lack of success all those years.

The Red Sox would appear in the World Series in 1946, 1967 and 1975 losing all three World Series. In 1986, it looked like the Curse would finally be broken.

The Red Sox started on the road at Shea Stadium and won the first game 1-0 as Bruce Hurst and Calvin Schiraldi shutout the Mets on four hits and five walks. Jim Rice would score the only run of the game for Boston after he led off the seventh inning with a walk, went to second on a wild pitch and scored when Rich Gedman bounced into an error by Mets second baseman, Tim Teufel.

Game Two would also be won by the Red Sox. The final score was 9-3. Dwight Evans and Dave Henderson would hit home runs for the Sox. It appeared to me that there would probably be no World Series game in New York City when I would be there with my niece as the Red Sox were going back to Boston for the next three games of the Series. All they needed to do was win two of those games and the Curse would be broken and I would have no conflict that Saturday in New York City.

Surprisingly, though, the Mets would win Game Three handily by a 7-1 score. They would win Game Four by a 6-2 score. Game Five would be won by the Red Sox but it didn't matter to me. I was going to be in a city where there was a World Series game. Only one problem, I promised my niece a big weekend in the Big Apple.

This trip was also not setting well with a woman I had been dating that year. My girlfriend was hot to get married and I wasn't. There were just enough issues and differences in our relationship that made me think that marriage would not be an option. Our relationship was tenuous at best. I had been practicing family law for six years by that time which also didn't help my attitude towards marriage. Yet, the fact that we attended four of our friends weddings that year seemed to create additional pressure to consider marriage.

If there weren't enough issues between us before I took this trip to New York City with my niece, there was one now, namely, the trip to New York City with my niece. My girlfriend didn't understand why she wasn't invited. Strangely, she also took exception to the fact that my niece and I were going to share a hotel room. Obviously, the relationship was on its last legs and would not last much longer after I returned to Tampa from the trip.

I had reservations for a room at the Hotel Edison. It was an older hotel, but nice, at least I thought so, and was in the Theater District in New York City and at a rate that wouldn't break me financially. I arrived there on Friday afternoon, checked in and rested for a moment on the bed. I was going to have to go back to the airport to meet Nancy. However, I fell asleep only to wake up at about the time her plane arrived. I hustled to the airport and found Nancy and we headed back to the hotel room.

I knew I wanted to go to the World Series game the next night but wasn't sure how to bring the subject up, so I didn't. Nancy and I went to see a musical, 42nd Street, and then ate dinner afterward at Mamma Leone's restaurant. We spent the rest of Friday evening at Rosie O'Grady's Saloon.

Although my niece was born outside Cleveland, my sister and brother-in-law, Rose and Ray, moved to Orlando, Florida when Nancy was very young. For those of you familiar with central Florida in the 1980s, there was an entertainment district known as Church Street Station in downtown Orlando.

The centerpiece was Rosie O'Grady's Good Time Emporium. That Rosie O'Grady's featured a jazz band. Rosie O'Grady's Saloon in New York City was very different. To me, it was how I envisioned being in Dublin, Ireland. The people, the music, the decor was pure Ireland.

Saturday morning came and Nancy and I went out to breakfast in Greenwich Village. I thought I would run her around a lot and make her tired so that she wouldn't mind if I went to the World Series game. We also went to the United Nations, Battery Park and to the top of the World Trade Center. Soon after that, I would drop the bomb on my niece that I was going to go the World Series and since I would have to get a ticket from a scalper, the ticket would be expensive.

Obviously, I didn't handle it well and I did ask my niece to contribute to this section:

Our trip to NY. Hmm. We were staying in a scary looking hotel. I think the nails were sticking up out of the floor molding as we walked in the doorway – which was the first sign that something was awry. The second, of course, was being left in the hotel all by myself to watch MY team (I was living in Boston at the time, going to BU) get slaughtered by those damned Mets. I'm not even sure I knew you were going to the game without me. Did you go out to get tickets and then decide to go at it alone? I think that might be the case, but honestly can't remember. Anyhow, talk about feeling alone. MY team had come so close only to lose it by one simple ball rolling through the first baseman's legs, and yet there was not a single soul in New York City I could commiserate with! So, I went to bed and woke up (what seemed like) hours later with a severe case of bed head, to a ringing telephone. Did I want to go check out the Irish Bar, you asked. Uh, are you crazy!!! - I replied. Or at least I did inside. My thoughts – you dumped me, left me for hours alone in a crappy hotel in New York City (which, now that I'm a grown-up, I'm sure cost an arm & a leg), and now you want me to go out. Have you even seen my bed head? We eventually made it to the Irish Bar (another night) and had a lot of fun. I (eventually) forgave you for dumping me, and now we have a great story to tell. ;-)

After leaving the hotel to go to the game, I took the subway to Shea Stadium to look for a ticket for the game. I wasn't sure I would find one and was half thinking about what Nancy and I could do if I didn't get a ticket. While on the subway on the way over to the stadium, I got a stopped by a police officer. I was carrying my camera under my jacket and it had a telescopic lens. I suppose the officer thought it could have been a gun so I showed it to him.

Surprisingly, when I got outside Shea Stadium, I ran into a guy who said he was a firefighter and he wanted to sell a ticket. I paid $80 for it which I thought was a bargain. I had money left over to buy a souvenir World Series T Shirt. The ticket was a good seat in one of the front rows in the upper deck along the left field line. One thing I learned about World Series games since then, especially up north, is that many people don't like sitting out in the cold weather in October, especially at night, to see a baseball game, even if it is the

World Series. Looking back, I'm not surprised that I was able to get a ticket so reasonably priced.

Baseball fans know that Game Six was a memorable game. At least one movie was made about it and numerous books were written about it. The game wasn't that well played and was probably entertaining for that reason. I remember Roger Clemens pitched four innings of no-hit ball and he left the game earlier than I thought he should have.

The game on the field would not compare to what I soon witnessed. It may be the strangest thing I ever saw at a baseball game.

While watching the play on the field, something floating in the sky caught my eye. When I looked to see what it was, it turned out to be a guy parachuting into the stadium with a "Let's Go Mets" sign. (Imagine this happening post 9/11 at a game in New York City) It was a very enthusiastic fan and his name was Michael Sergio. He eventually went to jail for contempt for refusing to identify the pilot who flew him over the stadium that night so he could parachute into the game.

He never did testify who the pilot was and eventually was released from jail and pardoned as his brother was dying of cancer. He was pardoned so he could spend time with his brother before he died.

As the game went on, it got colder but I hung in there. The game was tied up 3-3 after nine innings.

In the top of the tenth, Dave Henderson of the Red Sox led off with a home run off Rick Aguilera to give the Red Sox a 4-3 lead. After strikeouts to both Spike Owen and Calvin Schiraldi, Wade Boggs doubled to left field. Marty Barrett then singled him home to give the Red Sox a 5-3 lead. That's the way the tenth inning ended for the Red Sox.

All the Red Sox had to do was to hold the Mets to one run or less and they would win the World Series and finally bring an end to the Curse of the Bambino. So when Wally Backman and Keith Hernandez each flied out to start the bottom of the tenth, it looked especially promising for the Red Sox. It reminded me of a paragraph in the poem Casey at the Bat by Ernest Lawrence Thayer:

And then when Cooney died at first, and
Barrows did the same
A sickly silence fell upon the patrons of the game.
A straggling few got up to go in deep despair.
The rest Clung to that hope which springs
eternal in the human breast;
They thought, if only Casey could get but a
whack at that - We'd put up even money, now,
with Casey at the bat.

Just as in the poem, the next two batters reached base as Gary Carter singled and that was followed by Kevin Mitchell's single. The Mets had runners on first and second. Ray Knight would then hit a single and Carter would score. That made the score 5-4 with runners on first and third.

Bob Stanley was called in to replace Red Sox pitcher Calvin Schiraldi. Stanley then threw a wild pitch while pitching to Mookie Wilson. That tied the game when Mitchell scored from third. Ray Knight advanced to second base on the play.

Now, I don't know how long I'm going to live or if I'll get Alzheimer's Disease but I will always remember what happened next until one of those events occur. It would be impossible to forget about the play as I see it replayed over and over during every World Series broadcast.

Mookie Wilson hit a little grounder up the first base line. An easy play for the first baseman, Bill Buckner. My first thought was, great, now the game is going into additional extra innings and I was getting colder.

However, Buckner failed to pick up the ball and it rolled through his legs and Knight scored from second with the winning run. When I saw the ball go through his legs, I thought Mookie could run forever as the ball harmlessly dribbled into right field. He didn't need to as the Mets won the game, tying the series 3-3.

I don't recall a stadium erupting as Shea Stadium did afterward. For me, it was a baseball high. I couldn't wait to get back to the hotel and see if I could get Nancy to go out and eat. I didn't realize that it was 12:20 am. I didn't get back to the hotel until well after 1:00 am. I remember that Nancy was in no mood to go out and eat with me. I went out to eat anyway. There was no way I could fall asleep easily after witnessing this game.

I went to the Brasserie in New York City. Whatever I ate I am sure it was great. I don't recall what Nancy and I did for breakfast the next morning but she caught her plane and went back to Boston. I left on Monday.

It was pouring rain Sunday and I knew Game Seven would probably be postponed and it was. I did see an older man with his son or grandson at a restaurant where I was eating. They were wearing Red Sox jackets and I got the impression that they were in town for the World Series. I felt bad for them as they would have to pay for an extra night in New York City to see Game Seven which was rescheduled for Monday night.

My impression was that after losing Game Six the way they did, the Red Sox would have difficulty coming back to win Game Seven. However, the Red Sox took a 3-0 lead after five innings but the Mets tied the game with three runs in the sixth and they scored three more runs in the seventh inning.

The Red Sox would make it close by scoring two runs in their top of the eighth inning but the Mets would score two runs in the bottom of the eighth inning and win the game 8-5 and win the World Series.

It would be the Mets' second World Series championship. They haven't won the World Series since then. For the Red Sox, the Curse of the Bambino continued. The Curse would finally be broken when they won the World Series in 2004.

They won the World Series again in 2007. (They would be down three games to one to my Indians in the American League Championship series in 2007 but won three straight to get into the World Series.)

A few other things about Game Six. I don't remember this but apparently the Mets put on the scoreboard in the Tenth Inning "Congratulations Boston Red Sox, World Champions." Also, the Red Sox dressing room was dressed up with plastic to protect the lockers and the players' clothes from the inevitable celebration.

Champagne was brought in for the celebration. When the game ended as abruptly as it did and the Red Sox lost, people were taking that stuff down and removing the champagne as quickly as they could.

Sadly, in February 2012, one of the heroes of that game, Gary Carter, passed away from brain cancer after fighting the cancer for ten months. He was 57. He had the two out single that started the Mets rally in the tenth inning in Game Six. Gary Carter made his major league debut with the Montreal Expos in 1974 and played through 1992 when he would also finish his career with the Expos. He also played for the Mets, Giants and Dodgers during those years.

Gary Carter always seemed to be one of the decent players during his career and had excellent statistics. He was elected to baseball's Hall of Fame in 2003. He would be the first player who played in Game Six who would pass away.

Me playing the piano. I would not become the great pianist that my Mom would have liked. The Cleveland Indians belt might be a clue why.

Mom and I at a game at Jacobs Field in 2001. This time the Indians did not give her a can of deodorant.

Niece Nancy on top of the World Trade Center in October, 1986. Little did she know that she would be alone in New York City that night.

Scott Robinson dressed as a blind umpire when I first met him. He would become an inspiration to myself and many other people who know him.

Sam Jethroe, left, in his Cleveland Buckeyes
uniform. He would be National League Rookie of
the Year in 1950 at the age of 33. Most baseball
fans missed seeing his best years.

Ray Chapman, right, the only major league player
killed by a pitched baseball (Wikimedia commons)

My camouflage jersey, left

1871 Cleveland Forest Citys, right
(Wikimedia commons)

Municipal Stadium being torn down. Too bad there was not a more dignified way for it to be demolished.

Friendly Cleveland faces, Jimmy and Rachel, greet Indians fans after games.

CHAPTER EIGHT

Seventh Inning

At the start of the Rangers seventh inning, the Indians brought in a left hand relief pitcher, Nick Hagadone. Ian Kinsler led off the inning with a single that dropped in front of Shelley Duncan in left field. Elvis Andrus hit a hard line drive to Choo in right field who made a great catch for the first out.

With Josh Hamilton at the plate, Kinsler got caught off first base when Hagadone threw over on a pickoff attempt. Kinsler ran towards second where Santana threw the ball to Cabrera who tagged him out. Hamilton then struck out swinging.

Derek Holland was still pitching for the Rangers and came into the bottom of the seventh inning having thrown 82 pitches. The Indians did not challenge Holland in the seventh as Choo grounded out to the first baseman, Duncan struck out and Hannahan grounded out shortstop to first.

Jack Hannahan, like most baseball players, spent a significant amount of time in the minor leagues before playing with the Tribe in 2012. He started his career in 2001 but didn't play in the major leagues until 2006 when he appeared in three games for the Detroit Tigers. The minor leagues, of course, are where almost all major league players spend time improving their skills while the team they are under contract with decides whether they have a future at the major league level.

I enjoy minor league baseball games and most of the 89 baseball stadiums where I have attended professional games are minor league stadiums. Living in Cleveland, there are many minor league teams within a reasonable driving distance. Four of these teams are affiliated with the Cleveland Indians which makes it easy for fans like myself to go and watch these players as they grow through the Indians system.

On any given day, I can drive to see the Akron Aeros, Columbus Clippers, Mahoning Valley Scrappers and Lake County Captains play. Also within driving distance are the Erie Seawolves and Toledo Mudhens which are Detroit Tiger affiliates.

In recent years, independent minor league teams have become popular and the Lake Erie Crushers are located just west of Cleveland in Avon and are in the independent Frontier League.

When I lived in Tampa before the Devil Rays arrived, I would attend Florida State League games. The Florida State League is referred to as a high-A level minor league which is three levels below the major league. As a fan, it's exciting to see someone play at those levels who you can tell will make it to the major league level.

The first player who fit this description was Gary Redus. He played for the Tampa Tarpons which was a Cincinnati Reds affiliate in 1980. I was impressed by his play in games at Al Lopez Field in Tampa. That year he would play the whole season in Tampa and bat .301 with 16 home runs, 68 runs batted in and 50 stolen bases.

Two years later, he would be playing for the Cincinnati Reds in the first year of what would be a 13 year major league career. What I remember most about Al Lopez Field was the curved metal roof that would clang every time a foul ball landed on it.

Another minor league player I remember being impressed with was Frank "Big Hurt" Thomas. I saw him play in Columbus, Georgia against the Columbus Catfish in 1990 when he was with the Birmingham Barons, a White Sox affiliate in the Southern League, a AA level minor league.

In the game against the Catfish, Thomas appeared to effortlessly hit two balls off the outfield wall for doubles. He outclassed the other players on the field. It was surprising to still see him playing at that level as it was in the summer and the White Sox were in the middle of a pennant race and needed his bat. He was called up to Chicago soon after I saw him play and he batted .330 in 60 games for the White Sox during the rest of the 1990 season.

More recently, I had the opportunity to see Stephen Strasburg pitch in 2010 for the Syracuse Chiefs of the International League, a AAA level minor league. He looked impressive although he gave up the first home run of his professional career to Rene Rivera of the Scranton/Wilkes-Barre Yankees. Two weeks later, Strasburg would be pitching here in Cleveland for the Washington Nationals.

Another Nationals' star I saw play in the minor leagues was Bryce Harper. In 2011, I saw him play for the Harrisburg Senators in Erie against the Seawolves. I captured a continuous picture of him hitting a Home Run.

Before the game, he came out and signed autographs for the fans. He knew he was the reason that many fans came out to the game. He had been a highly touted amateur player who was the first selection in the 2010 baseball draft. He would become Washington National teammates with Stephen Strasburg who was the first selection in the 2009 baseball draft.

I sat next to an employee of the Seawolves whose job it was to chronicle every ball that Harper either hit or touched. However, they did forget to put someone outside the park to get the home run ball that Harper hit over the right field wall and onto Holland Street.

There are many interesting promotions at minor league games that the major league teams would probably not be caught dead using. The Seawolves, at one game, gave away six new compact fluorescent light bulbs to every fan. They were easily worth more than the cost of the ticket.

In Colorado Springs, one of the friendlier cities that I have visited, the fans at a Sky Sox game were asked to sing the Kit Kat theme song between one of the innings and there was a competition between the first base side and the third base side. Not sure who won. But everyone likes free candy. I remember the fan sitting next to me buying me a beer when he learned I was a tourist there to see the game. Everybody likes free beer, too.

One thing about minor league baseball games is that the seats are closer to home plate so the fans have to be especially careful when a batted ball is hit so as not to get struck by a foul ball.

A favorite minor league memory was in 1993 at the Florida State League All Star Game at Al Lang Stadium in St. Petersburg. I had a seat close to the field. Al Lang Stadium is a fabulous place to see a baseball game. It is along Tampa Bay in St. Petersburg and you can see sailboats gliding by and there is also a little airport for small private planes nearby. The ball park is surrounded by palm trees which gives it the appearance of a tropical setting. It is a relaxing and serene setting to see a ball game.

At the All Star game, in the bottom of the eighth inning, Daytona Beach Cubs outfielder, Bernie Nunez, was batting against Ben Weber, a right hand pitcher for the Dunedin Blue Jays. My seat was along the first base line and Bernie hit the ball high in the air into foul territory along the first base line and it appeared to be coming in my direction and, as the ball kept spinning, came right to me.

I would like to say that I caught it but I muffed it. However, the ball landed right below my seat and I grabbed it. At the end of the game, I caught Bernie's attention as he was leaving the field to get him to autograph it.

He told me to wait a minute. He went into the dugout and brought out the bat that he hit the ball with. He cracked the bat hitting the ball foul and handed the bat to me. I could not have been more appreciative. As much as I'm starting to get rid of some of my baseball memorabilia, this ball and bat will probably be with me until I pass away. He autographed the baseball. I also got the pitcher who threw the pitch to sign it.

I sent a letter to the management of the Daytona Cubs telling them what Bernie did and how much I appreciated it. They responded with a letter acknowledging how decent a person Bernie was. Unfortunately for Bernie, 1993 was to be his last year in the affiliated minor leagues. He never played higher than the AA level and in the late 1990s; he would be playing in the independent minor leagues.

The pitcher, Ben Weber, was just starting his career and pitched professionally through 2006. He would pitch in 228 major league games from 2000 through 2005. He compiled a 19-8 Won Loss record during that time with seven saves. His best years were with the Anaheim Angels from 2000 through 2003.

Minor league games are also a place to see major league players on rehabilitation assignments. In 1982, also at Al Lang Stadium, I went to see J.R. Richard pitch for the Daytona Beach Astros against the St. Petersburg Cardinals. J.R. Richard was one of the great pitchers in the major leagues throughout the 1970s.

He pitched his whole major league career with the Houston Astros. In 1978 and 1979 he had over 300 strikeouts in each of those seasons and led the National League both years in that category. In July

1980 he suffered a stroke and collapsed before an Astros game and had to have emergency surgery.

He was unable to return to his major league form afterward and was sent to the minors to work his way back to the majors. He looked great when I saw him pitch against the St. Petersburg Cardinal batters. He had success in the Florida State League with a 3-1 Win Loss record and a 2.79 ERA. However, after being promoted to the AAA Tucson Toros, his earned run average ballooned to 13.68. He never did make it back to the majors.

The story got worse. A business deal went bad and cost him over $300,000 and he paid his Wife $669,000 in a divorce case. After being married and divorced again and losing his home and most of his money, J.R. found himself sleeping under an overpass in Houston. It appears that his life has returned to normal after turning to a local church for help.

Although not a rehabilitation case, another major league player I saw play in the minor leagues was Steve Howe. In 1987, I saw Steve Howe pitch for the Oklahoma City 89ers at War Memorial Stadium in Buffalo, New York, home of the Buffalo Bisons. These teams were in the AAA level American Association.

Steve Howe was a great pitcher. In the game against the Bisons, he picked two runners off of first base. Like the other minor league players I mentioned, Howe outclassed the other players on the field. Why wasn't he playing in the major leagues? He was serving one of his seven major league suspensions for drug abuse.

Howe was plagued with drug and alcohol problems throughout his life and was one of two major league players eventually banned for life because of substance abuse problems. He played in the major leagues again after that, for the New York Yankees from 1994 through 1996, after winning an appeal over his lifetime ban. 1996 was the last year Howe pitched in the major leagues. He died in a car accident in 2006 and tests showed that he had methamphetamine in his system. He was 48.

Another reason I like minor league baseball is that I have met some of the nicest fans attending the games. I met one of the nicest people, and a fellow baseball junkie, at a minor league game in Charleston, West Virginia in 2009. It was a Friday and I remember the place being crowded with almost a "happy hour" atmosphere. The game was at Appalachian Power Park. It is a new park, built in 2005 for the West Virginia Power minor league team, and has an interesting landmark, a cemetery on a hill overlooking the stadium.

The West Virginia Power is a lower A level minor league affiliate of the Pittsburgh Pirates and is in the South Atlantic League.

There were celebrities there that night. Spongebob was there as well as West Virginia University's musket-carrying mascot, Rebecca Durst. She was the second female mascot in Mountaineer history. (The term referring to her as a mascot is theirs and not mine.)

More interesting were the fans. Many fans along the third base line brought duck umbrellas and opened them every time a foul ball headed their way as they would yell "duck." Another fan brought a toaster and would put bread in the toaster when an opposing player had two strikes on him and the fan would tell the batter that he was toast. He would then pass the toast out if the batter struck out.

But the fan I was most impressed with was dressed as a blind umpire. His name is Scott Robinson. He would be someone that I would find inspirational.

Scott and I would become baseball buddies and I would see him periodically over the next few years. Scott is about 20 years younger than me and has a wonderful wife and two great children. If you were to meet Scott, you would not think that he had a care in the world.

Since I met him, I have seen him here in Cleveland numerous times at the Cleveland Clinic. He has had to come up here to get his body prepared for a heart transplant.

Now, I'm 61 years old and have never spent a night in the hospital and cannot imagine having to go through numerous operations just for the opportunity to have a heart transplant. I certainly cannot imagine myself being able to go through the process and remain upbeat. So, whenever I have a problem or an issue that might cause me to be anxious or upset, I think about Scott and how his issues are much more serious than whatever is bothering me at the time.

It helps to wear the A Heart for Scotty D bracelet to remind me to keep any problems that I might have in perspective. He has told me many interesting stories from his childhood when he started to become a baseball junkie.

When Scott was a youngster, he lived near Watt Powell Park which is the previous minor league stadium where the Charleston baseball teams played. Since he didn't have much money when he was a kid, he would ride his bicycle to the stadium and hang around outside chasing batting practice balls, home runs balls and foul balls that cleared the stadium walls.

His favorite times at the park were the Sundays when his dad took him to ball games. That may be why his life turned out a little more normal than mine.

The stadium where he attended games, and eventually worked, was named after Watt Powell who was born in West Virginia and played minor league baseball from 1906 through 1910 in the Class C Virginia League and worked his way up to the San Francisco Seals of the Pacific Coast League. After he returned to Charleston, Powell helped construct the stadium that eventually carried his name. Every Opening Day for the Charleston team, Scott places a baseball on Watt Powell's grave.

Scott became the batboy for the minor league team and has great stories about his time as a batboy from 1988 through 1990. During the games, as part of his job, Scott would try to grab foul balls that would hit the screen behind the plate and would receive cheers or boos whether he did this successfully or not. As he told me, for someone who didn't play any sports, it was nice to have the crowd react, good or bad, to his hustle.

He also had opportunities to shag batting practice fly balls and hang around with the players, some of whom would make it to the Major Leagues. Another story of Scott's that I can relate to is when he told me that he received flack from his schoolmates who thought being a batboy for the minor league team was lame. Similarly, my schoolmates thought going to Indians games was just a waste of time during my last couple of years in high school.

Scott was a batboy for the Charleston Wheelers who were a Cubs affiliate in the South Atlantic League during the 1988 and 1989 seasons and a Reds affiliate in 1990. However, sad to say, Scott's discipline and hustle did little to inspire those teams as the 1988 team finished with a 51-86 record, the 1989 team finished in last place with a 58-76 record and the 1990 team finished in third place with a 77-66 record.

CHAPTER NINE

Eighth Inning

In the eighth inning, Hagadone induced Michael Young to ground out shortstop to first. A right handed batter, Craig Gentry, was called upon to pinch hit for David Murphy. Gentry popped out to the first baseman. Nelson Cruz then grounded out to the third baseman.

In the Indians half of the eighth inning, Derek Holland struck out Lou Marson to begin the inning. Michael Brantley and Jason Kipnis hit back to back singles to put runners on first and third. Right handed relief pitcher, Mike Adams, was brought into the game to relieve Holland. For the first time in the game, the Tribe had two runners on base with less than two outs. At this time, on cue, John Adams started his rhythmic drumming on his bass drum which spurred on the crowd which started clapping along in unison.

With a one strike count, Asdrubal Cabrera doubled down the first base line scoring Brantley. Kipnis stopped at third base. Carlos Santana came to bat and the Rangers infield played in to try to get an out at home if Santana hit a ground ball.

With a one ball, one strike count, Mike Adams threw a fast ball to Santana who swung and missed the pitch. The catcher, Mike Napoli, was unable to catch the pitch which got by him. Kipnis scored from third and Cabrera advanced to third base.

It was scored a passed ball. These two runs were all the runs the Tribe was able to get that inning as Santana would strike out swinging. Travis Hafner, batting next, broke his bat while hitting a ground ball out to the first baseman.

As I mentioned earlier, when I arrived at the game tonight, the Indians were giving away a Chris Perez replica jersey. It is not unusual for teams to give away items to attract people to ball games but what has changed over the years is that the teams have sponsors provide the items. This saves the team from having to pay for the giveaways and provides advertisement for the sponsor of the product. Tonight's sponsor was Cleveland's newspaper, the Plain Dealer.

I am proud to say that for about four years from the time I was 12 to 16 I delivered the Plain Dealer to my neighbors in Lorain, Ohio.

I still have the bag that they gave us paperboys with the reflective lettering to carry the newspapers. Now, as a sign of changing times, people deliver the newspaper for a living.

This particular evening, I don't take the item the team was giving away. As I usually go out after the game to eat or drink, I hate to carry the giveaway with me. This night was no different. Also, as the jersey has the name of the advertiser on it, the jersey does not look all that authentic.

One thing about being a big baseball fan is that people buy me baseball related gifts for holidays and give me their unwanted baseball items. I usually don't mind the gifts I receive but they are not always items that I treasure. Some gifts do stand out.

The most generous gift I ever received was from my Aunt Ruby, my Mom's sister. In 1962, my Mom, my sister Barbara and I took the Aquarama, a ferry that ran from Cleveland to Detroit, to visit Aunt Ruby, Uncle Eric and cousins Joanie and Suzie. My cousin Denis was out of the country at the time.

My Aunt gave me two corrugated boxes full of baseball, football, basketball, hockey and non-sports cards that were collected by my cousin Denis from 1949 through 1958. He was my Aunt Ruby and Uncle Eric's only son and oldest child.

There were a few thousand cards in the two boxes and the boxes were heavy, bulky and difficult to carry. Along with my little suitcase, I had to drag these boxes back home with me on the Aquarama.

Once I got the boxes home and saw what was in them, it was like finding a lost treasure chest. If given an option of choosing the boxes with these cards or boxes of gold, it would have been an easy decision, definitely the cards.

As I mentioned, the cards had been collected by my cousin Denis. Sadly, he would die in 1964 when he was just 20 years old. Until I wrote this book, I thought I was given the cards after he passed away. Cousins Joanie and Suzie told me otherwise.

It turns out that I reminded my Aunt of Denis and she wanted me to have the cards. She also probably wanted them out of her house. I have always treated the cards with a certain reverence as it was a connection to a past that I was too young to recall. Some of the cards featured players from teams that had relocated including the St. Louis Browns, Philadelphia Athletics, Brooklyn Dodgers and others. The jewel of the collection was the 1951 Bowman Mickey Mantle.

It is Mantle's true rookie card although many collectors consider the 1952 Topps to be his rookie card. Years later, I would trade the football, hockey and non-sports cards from that collection for the 1951 Bowman Willie Mays rookie card and some cash.

I later traded off the basketball cards. The baseball cards are still in my possession and are complemented by the baseball cards my Dad would bring me home when he picked up his six pack from Mary's Deli and Grocery Store on Oberlin Avenue and West Ninth Street in Lorain every night, including Sunday when alcohol sales were against the law.

A pack of cards cost a nickel then. I collected baseball cards from 1959 through 1965. I never considered the cards to be an investment. Collecting cards was always a hobby to me. However, as I am getting older, I have started to streamline the collection. I still buy cards having started collecting again in 1979.

Another interesting item that I received from a friend was a little souvenir baseball bat. While I was still living in Tampa, a friend of mine would dumpster dive for a hobby. That involves going through other peoples' trash. He brought me a little wooden souvenir baseball bat that he found while dumpster diving. Imprinted into the bat were the numbers 6-20-76 and under that was an imprint B'NAI B'RITH and under that was imprinted BILL VEECK.

What made the bat intriguing were three signatures on the end of the bat which were covered by plastic wrap. The signatures were those of Hank Greenberg, Howard Cosell and Bill Veeck.

These three were Jewish men associated with baseball. Hank Greenberg was a great baseball player for the Tigers and Pirates from 1930 through 1947. After his career as a ballplayer, he would be hired by the Indians and become the team's General Manager.

The man that hired him was Bill Veeck who owned the Indians during the late 1940s. He was the owner of the Indians in 1948 which was the last year the Indians won the World Series. He would have to sell the team to help pay for his divorce settlement the next year. (I sometimes wonder if the team would have won more championships had Veeck not gone through a divorce.)

Veeck will also always be remembered as the owner who signed Larry Doby to play for the Indians. Doby was the first African American baseball player in the American League and the second in the majors behind Jackie Robinson.

The third signature belonged to Howard Cosell. He would be remembered to most people as an announcer on ABC's Monday Night Football during the shows infancy. Before that, he was best known as a boxing announcer and did some baseball announcing later in his career.

I remember receiving another interesting item. This one was from prison. As I mentioned in the introduction, I represented a woman who received the death penalty. It was the first time a woman received the death penalty in Tampa. Her name is Carla Caillier.

In 1986, Carla and her husband were living in Louisiana and he was having difficulty finding work so he moved to Tampa. He was working and sending money back to Carla to support her and their child.

Back home in Louisiana, Carla started seeing a man. His name was Ty Payne. Payne took a bus to Tampa. He then located Carla's husband and shot him in cold blood. The gunshot wounds were fatal. After Payne got caught, he told investigators that Carla was also involved in planning and preparing her husband's murder with him.

She was extradited from Louisiana and had a lawyer from there come to Tampa to represent her. In cases like this, the law required a Florida attorney to be listed as counsel of record and participate in the trial. I was asked by the local bar association if I would do that, so I did. Carla was eventually found guilty as the jury believed she assisted Ty Payne by planning with him and preparing him for the murder of her husband.

The jury recommended life imprisonment but Judge Harry Coe III overruled the jury and gave

Carla the death penalty. The Supreme Court of Florida reduced her punishment to life imprisonment with no possibility of parole for at least 25 years.

While the trial was pending in Tampa, I often talked to Carla when she was in jail. It must have become obvious to her that I was a big baseball fan. I had minimal contact with her after her trial in 1987 and after she went off to prison.

All I knew about Carla was that while she was in prison she was receiving religious counseling from a local minister. Later he was charged with smuggling escape tools into the prison to her.

Out of the blue, I got a letter from her from prison in 2000. She sent me a note with a magazine ad that showed new post office stamps featuring baseball players. That was about the only contact I had with her after her trial and I haven't heard from her since.

The Judge in her case, Harry L. Coe III, was a professional baseball player at one time. He was a pitcher in Detroit's minor league system from 1953 through 1956 and reached the AAA level.

He also earned money pitching for the Tampa Tarpons in 1957 and 1958. The Tarpons were a Class D affiliate of the Philadelphia Phillies in the Florida State League. He only pitched home games as he was attending law school at Stetson Law School in Gulfport, Florida which is outside St. Petersburg.

Coe was an excellent pitcher, compiling a 44-15 Win Loss record in the two years that he pitched for the Tarpons.

His life would end tragically as he committed suicide in 2000 and the suicide would be linked to a gambling addiction. I always found Judge Coe to be friendly and approachable and I remember a brief conversation with him about minor league baseball in Tampa. We agreed to meet again to talk about the subject more. It never happened. It was a lesson to me not to let opportunities to meet with people get delayed.

In that brief conversation, I did ask him who the first African-American baseball player to play on the Tampa minor league team was and he told me it was Jimmy Wynn.

Wynn played for the Tampa Tarpons in 1962 but, otherwise, I have not been able to confirm that he was the first African-American to play baseball for the Tarpons.

A final story about baseball players and court. I was making an appearance for a client in criminal court one day in Tampa. Attorneys were allowed to sit in chairs along the wall while waiting for their cases to be called. They would bring prisoners out and sit them in these chairs too.

On one occasion, I found myself sitting next to Darryl Strawberry who was in jail for some pending criminal charges. He played right field for the New York Mets in Game 6 and it took all my self control not to start talking about that game with him. The Judge was real strict about talking in the Courtroom while cases were going on.

His friend and former teammate with both the Yankees and the Mets, Dwight Gooden, was there to offer his support. Both were Tampa residents.

Finally, readers should be forewarned. I have been know to take baseball items from people who don't know what the items are, especially if I'm afraid the items will be discarded or unappreciated.

I had a client come into my office once with an autographed baseball and had no idea where he got it or who signed it. As he wasn't a baseball fan, it did not seem very valuable to him. I basically confiscated it from him and told him that I was going to keep it since it appeared that he had no appreciation for the ball.

The baseball has a USO stamp on it. All the players who autographed the ball have one thing in common, they all played in the major leagues in 1979. There are eleven signatures on it including Rico Carty, John Stearns, Bobby Tolan and eight others. One signature I cannot identify. If anyone knows anything about this ball, please feel free to contact me.

CHAPTER TEN

Ninth Inning

Right hand relief pitcher, Vinnie Pestano, came in from the bullpen running at full speed to pitch the ninth inning for the Indians.

The first batter he faced was Mike Napoli who struck out swinging. The next batter he faced was the left handed designated hitter, Mitch Moreland. The Indians shifted three infielders to the right side of the infield but Moreland singled a ground ball through the shift anyway.

Alberto Gonzalez then hit a fly ball to center fielder Michael Brantley for the inning's second out. Ian Kinsler came to bat. He swung and missed the first pitch, a fast ball.

The second pitch was a slider which Kinsler watched go by that was called strike two. Kinsler fouled off the next pitch but then struck out swinging at a 91 miles per hour fast ball for the final out of the inning.

Right handed pitcher, Alexi Ogando, came in to pitch for the Rangers in the ninth inning. He and I share the same birthday, October 5th. Shin-Soo Choo led off the 9th inning for the Indians and after swinging and missing the first two pitches, both 97 miles per hour fast balls, he took the next two pitches for balls. After fouling off another fast ball,

Choo hit a 98 miles per hour pitch for a single into right field. The fans let out their "Chooooooo" cheer. Johnny Damon was summoned to pinch hit for Shelley Duncan. He popped out to the third baseman.

Jack Hannahan, a left hand batter, came to bat and faced a shift where three fielders were on the right side of the infield. He hit a sharp grounder to the first baseman who tagged first base and threw to the third baseman, Alberto Gonzalez, who was covering second base. He tagged out Choo sliding into second base for a double play. The game went into extra innings.

I usually stay until the end of games. I started that habit after witnessing the comeback in Game 6 of the 1986 World Series. This policy was challenged on Opening Day of 2012 when the Indians hosted the Toronto Blue Jays.

It was April 5 and the high temperature that day was 46 degrees. The Indians had a 4-1 lead as the game went into the bottom of the ninth inning when Indians closer, Chris Perez, gave up three runs to allow the Blue Jays to tie the game.

The game would go 16 innings and last 5 hours and 14 minutes and end at 8:22 PM. The Blue Jays scored three runs in the top of the 16th to win the game.

As I mentioned earlier, I only remember my Dad taking me to two baseball games in Cleveland. He did take me to one other baseball game, the 1970 All Star Game in Cincinnati.

I graduated from Lorain High School in 1970 and decided to go to college at Eastern Kentucky University in Richmond, Kentucky. At the time, I thought I would like to be a police officer and went to Eastern to get a degree in Law Enforcement.

I wanted to visit the campus first and my Dad agreed to take me there for a visit. Dad had a high management position with Fruehauf Trailer Company and they had tickets for the 1970 All Star Game in Cincinnati which was on the way to our visit to Eastern. I planned the trip that way.

Dad was able to get tickets for the game. He took me and the worst that could happen to my Dad happened as the game went into extra innings, 12 innings to be exact.

I was amazed when I first saw the field at Riverfront Stadium. It had green artificial turf and the outline of the baseball diamond was painted onto the turf. The only areas of the infield that were dirt were the pitchers mound, three triangle areas, called sliding boxes, around the three bases and a circle where home plate and the batters boxes were. It was a typical of the stadiums that were built around the county in the early 1970s.

Later it would be referred to as a cookie cutter stadium as it was similar to all those other stadiums being built elsewhere at that time. Riverfront Stadium, like so many of the other stadiums built at the time, was designed for both baseball and football. A similar one was being built in Pittsburgh. Living in Cleveland, it was frustrating to see these nearby cities get new ball parks while we had the same old stadium. Of course, since then, both Cincinnati and Pittsburgh have new separate stadiums for baseball and football. Cleveland does too, now.

I do remember the game itself and do remember how frustrating it was to my Dad that it went extra innings. It turned out to be a bad day for the Cleveland Indians. (Another typical Cleveland experience.)

The Tribe's young All Star catcher, Ray Fosse, was bowled over in the bottom of the 12th inning by Pete Rose who scored the winning run on the play. Fosse was trying to block home plate to keep Rose from scoring. Fosse's right shoulder was separated on the play. His career was never the same after that game and it seemed that the Curse of Rocky Colavito continued.

The next day, I visited Eastern Kentucky University and my college career would start in August of 1970. I would not be a stranger to Riverfront Stadium after I started attending Eastern. I saw my first World Series game there in 1972. On Saturday, October 21, 1972, the sixth game of the World Series was being played up Interstate 75 from Richmond in Cincinnati. The Reds were hosting the Oakland A's.

On a lark, I decided to drive up to the game with a college buddy whose name I have long since forgotten. Baseball fans today would be surprised to know that this game was played during the day. We were able to get tickets at face value at the Will Call window. The tickets were available as someone notified the team that they would not be using their tickets.

Maybe it was not that surprising to get tickets in that manner as Saturday afternoons are for college football and I suspect some fans preferred to go to a football game that day. There were 52,737 fans at the game which was 3,300 fewer than would be there the next day for Game Seven.

The Reds were down 3 games to 2 in the series going into Game Six. The starting pitcher that day for the A's was left hander Vida Blue who was 24 years old. He started pitching in the majors at the age of 19 and had a Won Lost record of 24-8 in 1971 when he was just 21.

His earned run average in 1971 was 1.82. He had 8 complete game shutouts and struck out 301 batters. That was his first full year in the majors as a starting pitcher. Vida Blue started the 1972 season rejecting a contract offer from the A's owner, Charles O. Finley. What resulted was an ugly contract dispute that would not be resolved until late May.

Blue didn't pitch well after signing a contract and ended the season with a Win Loss record of 6-10 and out of the A's starting rotation. He was given a start in this sixth game of the World Series.

"Come on brother Vida" was a cheer heard at Riverfront Stadium from the few Oakland fans in attendance. Blue pitched well, giving up four hits, two walks and three earned runs in 5 2/3 innings to the Reds. One of the hits was a solo home run by Johnny Bench.

Reds pitchers, Gary Nolan, Ross Grimsley, Pedro Borbon and Tom Hall combined to only allow the A's one run on seven hits and one walk. The Reds won the game.

The World Series was tied three games each with the seventh and final game of the Series scheduled for the next day. Over 56,000 fans showed up the next day for Game 7 which was won by the Oakland A's by a final score of 3-2. The A's would also win the World Series in 1973 and 1974. The Reds would win the World Series in 1975 and 1976. Their 1975 Series opponents would be the Red Sox.

CHAPTER ELEVEN

Tenth Inning

Joe Smith came into the game to pitch the tenth inning for the Indians. The first batter he faced was Elvis Andrus. The first three pitches to Andrus were balls, the fourth was a strike but Andrus drew a walk on the next pitch. The next batter was Josh Hamilton. Hamilton flied out to the center fielder, Michael Brantley, for the first out.

The next batter was Michael Young. While Young was at bat, Andrus took off running from first and Young hit a fly ball for the second out to Choo in right field. Andrus apparently believed there were two outs and by the time he realized his mistake, he was thrown out before he could return to first base for a double play.

In the bottom of the tenth, Alexi Ogando pitched his second inning. The first batter to face him was Lou Marson who was batting .067. Ogando's earned run average was 0.66. Along with his .067 average, the scoreboard also pointed out that Marson had yet to hit a home run this year and had just one run batted in.

The first pitch was 81 miles per hour and Marson watched it go by for a strike. The second pitch was a ball, the third pitch was an 83 miles per hour strike that Marson watched go by and the final pitch was an 85 miles per hour strike that Marson watched go by for a called strike three.

Ogando then faced Michael Brantley. He also watched a strike go by, this time at 97 miles per hour. He swung and missed on the second pitch. After an inside pitch for a ball, he fouled off an 85 miles per hour pitch. He watched two 98 miles per hour pitches that were called balls go by which made the count 3-2 and then hit a deep fly ball to center field for the second out of the inning.

Jason Kipnis would not fare much better as he struck out to end the bottom of the tenth inning. These would be the only two innings Ogando would pitch and he reduced his earned run average to 0.61. He gave up one hit and struck out two batters in his two inning appearance.

The Indians would not provide any late inning heroics this evening. Many of the games I am writing about involve Indians games or minor league games but there was a time in my life that I probably saw more games at Tropicana Field in St. Petersburg than any other stadium.

I lived in Tampa from 1978 until I moved back to Cleveland in 2003. I was in Tampa during those years in the '80s and early '90s when groups in the Tampa area would try to bring major league baseball there. The groups would buy teams in other cities and announce that they were moving the teams to Tampa. Major League Baseball then stopped the teams from moving. (It is a right Major League Baseball has under their exemption to antitrust laws that was granted by the U.S. Supreme Court years ago.)

The result of the ownership groups threatening to move teams to Tampa was that those cities would build new baseball stadiums for the teams that the Tampa groups purchased. Finally, probably after all the new stadiums that could be built were, an expansion team was awarded to Tampa and the Devil Rays started play in 1998 to much fanfare.

I was a season ticket holder in their first year and probably saw 30 games that season. That was the only year I had a Devil Rays season ticket. I would still see a dozen games or so there each year after that until I moved back to Cleveland. As with an earlier expansion team in Miami, the Florida Marlins, it was predicted that the Florida baseball teams would attract large number of fans. That has not happened.

It seemed the only times the Devil Rays had good attendance were when they played against the New York Yankees or Boston Red Sox and fans of those teams living in the Bay area came to the game to root on those teams, often outnumbering the fans of the Devil Rays.

I remember calling the local radio sports show one Opening Day in Tampa when the host wanted to talk baseball. While on hold, I could hear the call before me. Honest to goodness, the caller before me wanted to talk about the Tampa Bay Buccaneers long snapper position. I couldn't believe it. All I could think of is that it is Opening Day, have some respect.

Both the Marlins and the Devil Rays (now just the Rays who dropped the Devil from their name a few years ago) have had disappointing attendance since they arrived on the scene. Nonetheless, I was a Devil Rays fan unless they were playing the Indians or the Braves, my two favorite teams. (I was a Braves fan as they were the "home" team as it was the closest major league team to Tampa while I lived there until the Devil Rays appeared on the scene.)

There was one game in particular at Tropicana Field that is worth writing about. It was May 11, 2002. The story of that game goes back to April 25th of that year. The Devil Rays were playing a Wednesday day game against Minnesota.

I attended that game with my buddy, Zach, who was a Minnesota native. The Rays came into that game with a 9-10 record and it looked like they would win the game and improve to 10-10. That would be a pretty good record for the Rays since the team still played like an expansion team.

I left after eight innings and the Devil Rays were leading 2-1. Their closer, Esteban Yan, was brought in to save the game in the top of the ninth inning. I was listening to the end of the game on the radio on my way to the class I had to teach that night. It didn't sound pretty as Yan gave up four runs in the top of the ninth and the Devil Rays lost 5-2. That was the first of 15 straight games they would lose.

With a 9-25 record, the only drama at the game that I attended on May 11 would be to see if they would lose their 16th game in a row.

It was a Saturday night and the Devil Rays were hosting the Baltimore Orioles. They lost to the Orioles the night before 6-5. Now as much as I like baseball, there are games that just bore me to tears and the night of May 11 was not much different.

The Devil Rays seem uninspired as the Orioles took a 4-0 lead into the bottom of the 5th inning when the Rays finally scored a run. They would score one more run in the bottom of the seventh inning to make the score 4-2. Towards the end of the game, I started gradually moving toward the exit.

The score was still 4-2 going into the bottom of the ninth inning. I was sitting high up in the right field stands so once the game ended, I could dart out to the parking lot and beat what little traffic there would be. The Orioles brought in their closer, Jorge Julio. The Devil Rays first batter, Jason Tyner, came in as a pinch hitter for Russ Johnson and singled. Chris Gomez would then get another single and the Devil Rays had runners on first and second with nobody out.

The next batter, John Flaherty, the Devil Rays catcher, would bunt into a force play at third base and Jared Sandberg would strike out. There were two men on first and second base but now two out. The next batter, Brent Abernathy, would single to right field and drive home a run and the Orioles lead would be reduced to 4-3.

The Devil Rays next batter was Randy Winn. He was one of my favorite Devil Rays players. Many of the players on the Devil Rays would probably not be in the major leagues if there had not been two additional teams added in 1998.

Many of the other Devil Rays players had previously played in the major leagues for other teams and their best years were behind them. Randy Winn was neither one of those. His primary major league baseball career was with the Devil Rays. He worked the count to 2-2 and then it happened.

He hit a game winning home run into the right center field stands. The 15 game winning streak was over and I was glad that I stayed until the end. This was the Devil Rays 35th game of the season and the first time they scored in the ninth inning. There were just a little over 10,000 people at that game and those there at the end were able to coax Randy Winn to come out for a curtain call.

CHAPTER TWELVE

Eleventh Inning

It's the eleventh inning and Joe Smith stayed on to pitch for the Indians. Craig Gentry, who pinch hit in the eighth inning, was the first batter to face Smith and drew a walk. Nelson Cruz then hit a ground ball that forced Gentry out at second base. The play should have been a double play but Asdrubal Cabrera dropped the ball while transferring it out of his glove. The failure to turn a double play would prove to be ruinous.

Strangely, the scoreboard listed the batter as the Indians' Michael Brantley and the fans start yelling at whoever was operating the scoreboard that the scoreboard was wrong. Mike Napoli came up to bat and hit a ground out to the third baseman and Nelson Cruz moved to second on the play. While Napoli was at bat, there was not a ball and strike count on the scoreboard and Jason Kipnis was listed as the batter.

With first base open, Indians manager Manny Acta, decided to intentionally walk Moreland, the next batter. After the intentional walk, Rangers manager Ron Washington sent up Adrian Beltre to pinch hit for Alberto Gonzalez. Beltre is usually the Rangers starting third baseman but had a sore left hamstring which is the reason he didn't start the game. It is unusual for a right hand batter to pinch hit against a right hand pitcher.

Beltre had never had a hit off of Smith in his career. Smith's first pitch to Beltre was a ball. The next pitch was a fast ball in the middle of the plate and Beltre hit the ball over the center field fence for a home run giving the Rangers a 5-2 lead. Ian Kinsler would then ground out to the shortstop to end the top of the eleventh inning.

For trivia fans, this was the first extra inning pinch hit home run against the Indians since 1977 when Brooks Robinson hit one in a game at Baltimore. It was the first extra inning pinch hit home run against the Indians in Cleveland since June 12, 1961 when Tribe pitcher Frank Funk gave up a two run pinch hit home run to Kansas City Athletics' Leo Posada in the top of the 10th inning. The Athletics went on to win that game 7-5.

In the bottom of 11th inning, the moon finally made an appearance through the cloudy sky. This happened to be the day that the Moon was the closest it would get to the Earth in 2012, 15,300 miles closer than on average.

Rangers closer Joe Nathan came in to pitch and the first batter he faced was Asdrubal Cabrera. Asdrubal would hit a single into right field on a 2-2 count.

Asdrubal would have four of the Indians' eight hits in this game. He would turn out to be one of two Indians picked to the American League All-Star team in 2012 along with closer Chris Perez.

Asdrubal would move to second on what is now referred to as defensive indifference. Carlos Santana would then bat and work a two ball no strike count but would strike out as would Travis

Hafner, the next batter. The Indians' last hope was Shin-Soo Choo who flied out to the right fielder to end the game.

The game took 3 hours and 12 minutes to complete and there were 21,307 fans there this evening.

"Moon River" was played on the public address system as the fans exited the game.

CHAPTER THIRTEEN

The Walk Home

I live downtown in Cleveland so part of the experience of going to the Indians games is the walk home, especially on a Saturday night. The first stop on my walk home is The Thirsty Parrot. The Parrot, as it is referred to by locals, is a bar and restaurant right across the street from Progressive Field. The Parrot is only open before, during and after sporting events in the Gateway District of Cleveland.

There is a large outdoor patio as well as an indoor seating area. The attraction for me is that one of my college students, Rachel, works there. The women who are serving this evening are dressed in Indians garb. Rachel is wearing a blue zippered Indians top and serves me a Coors Light. This first one is on Rachel.

Since Rachel is still attending school we talk briefly about her classes but the Parrot gets crowded quickly so she and Jimmy, who is the other outside server and also very friendly, have to start what will be a busy evening for them. The post game show is on the Parrot's television but other than me, I'm not sure anyone else is watching it.

After finishing my second beer, a Landshark (which I paid for), I then went out to eat on East 4th Street. East 4th Street is one block long and has restaurants on both sides of the street. The area is devoid of dance clubs, the types of which are located on West Sixth Street. East 4th is closed to vehicle traffic and most of the restaurants have open air seating along with indoor seating. After Indians games, this is one of the areas fans descend upon.

The area is illuminated by strings of lights which hang across the street. Periodically, one of the diners will see me walk by in my Indians garb and ask who won the game. I always find it odd when the psychics who work on East 4th Street ask me who won the game. You would think they would know.

East 4th Street is two blocks east of the Terminal Tower where the Horseshoe Casino recently opened. This area has grown over the past few years and the restaurants range from casual to fine dining.

Like most Saturday nights after Indians games, East 4th Street was crowded. One of my favorite places, Zocalo, a Mexican restaurant, was especially crowded this particular night as they were celebrating Cinco de Mayo. I was looking for a place to eat and ran into a buddy of mine, Carmine, and we decided to go to the Tilted Kilt which just opened up.

If you're not familiar with the Tilted Kilt, it is a sports bar where the servers are young women with low cut outfits, short skirts and bare midriffs. They also have men in kilts working there. The opening of the Kilt coincided with the opening of the Horseshoe Casino across the street. I got into the spirit of Cinco de Mayo by ordering a Dos Equis. In my mind, I'm the most interesting man in the world, so it was appropriate.

After eating there with Carmine, he and I went on our separate ways and I continued the walk back to my apartment. I took a different route than I did when I went to the game. The walk back home took me through Cleveland's Public Square which is the center of the city as it was platted out in 1796. Public Square appears in the movie "A Christmas Story" which was filmed in Cleveland.

Once every summer when I was a child, my Mom would build up her courage and drive from Lorain to Cleveland to take my sister Barbara and myself shopping for the school year. We shopped at Higbees which faced Public Square. Higbees closed in 1992 and the Horseshoe Casino now occupies that location.

There are a couple of prominent landmarks in Public Square that my walk takes me by. One is a statue of Moses Cleaveland dressed as a surveyor holding a staff in his right hand and a compass in his left hand. It was erected in 1888.

The other prominent landmark in Public Square is The Soldiers' and Sailors' Monument. The monument commemorates the Civil War and was completed in 1894. The prominent feature of the monument is a 125 foot tall column upon which stands the Goddess of Freedom. The base of the monument features four sculptures which depict Civil War battle scenes. Each sculpture represents the four main armed services at the time, the Cavalry, Infantry, Artillery and Navy.

Although the area has lost some glory over the years, I feel safe walking through the Square as the area is well lit with a police presence outside the casino.

As I continue on with my walk back home, I have to cross West 6th Street where this evening, I was able to resist its siren song. My favorite clubs, The Dive Bar and The Blind Pig would have to do without me until next Saturday night.

I did go to one more place, D'Vine Wine Bar, which is near my apartment. It is an upscale bar and restaurant, at least until I show up. D'Vine has always been one of my favorite hangouts as it is the closest bar to my apartment. It is a convenient place for me to go during the cold winter Cleveland nights. This particular evening I got to see favorite servers, Karen and Michelle. Then the evening was over for me and I went back to my apartment for the night.

CHAPTER FOURTEEN

The Camouflage Jersey

As I mentioned, I wear jerseys and hats that match what the Indians players are wearing when I attend games. However, there are a couple days a season when I wear patriotic baseball gear. I wear a red Indians hat with the block "C" which has red, white and blue stripes in it. I also wear an autographed, camouflage baseball jersey. I get asked about it a lot so here is the story. It includes another story of heartbreak.

On Saturday, September 1, 2001, when I was still living in Tampa, I went to Atlanta for a Braves game. They were hosting the Chicago Cubs. It was my last trip before 9/11. Former Indians star, Julio Franco, was playing first base for the Braves.

He was added to the team on the 1st as major league teams are allowed to expand their rosters up to 40 players on September 1st every year. Julio was 43 years old and had been playing professionally in the Mexican League when the Braves signed him to join them for the rest of the season which would include the playoffs.

Teams are allowed 25 players on their roster during the season but can add up to 15 more players for the last month. They seldom bring up that many players. For teams that are out of the pennant race, adding extra players is an opportunity to see how some of their minor league players can perform at the major league level.

Julio Franco is a favorite former player of those of us who are Cleveland Indians fans. He played eight seasons for the Indians. The Tribe traded Von Hayes, a highly regarded prospect, to the Philadelphia Phillies for five players in 1982 including Franco who was just 23 years old. The other players along with Franco that the Tribe received were Manny Trillo, George Vukovich, Jay Baller and Jerry Willard. Von Hayes would have a nice major league career but also be taunted regularly by a "Five for One" chant throughout his career.

I was surprised to see Julio playing that day as he had only played one game in the major leagues since 1997. Julio would continue to play in the Major Leagues until 2007 when he played in 15 games for the Braves. He retired from Major League Baseball when he was 49 years old.

The other memorable event in that game was the home run that Sammy Sosa hit off of Greg Maddux. In my naivety, I wanted to think that baseball players were not using performance enhancing drugs if they said they weren't. Sammy Sosa's home run hit the back wall of the Braves' bullpen on the fly. It was the longest home run hit at Turner Field. It was announced to be 471 feet.

Now, every year I went to Atlanta, I would also travel to Columbus, Georgia to see the Columbus Redstixx play at historic Golden Park. I referred to this park earlier having seen the Columbus Mudcats play there in 1990. These older minor league stadiums, I have learned, are always referred to as "historic." The Redstixx were the Cleveland Indians franchise in the South Atlantic League.

The SALLY league, as it is called, is what is referred to as a lower A level minor league. Players at that level have three levels of minor leagues above them that they would have to progress through before they would play in the major league.

I always liked visiting Columbus and Golden Park. Golden Park is nestled along a bend in the Chattahoochee River which separates Georgia and Alabama. I remember approaching the stadium one evening while driving across the bridge from Phenix City, Alabama. The stadium lights were on and the stadium appeared like a glowing jewel in the night.

Along the river runs the Chattahoochee RiverWalk. You can watch people jogging regularly along the RiverWalk. It is 15 miles long and connects Fort Benning to downtown Columbus. Many of the joggers looked like they were in the military and stationed at Fort Benning which is just east of the city.

I tried to rollerblade on the path once but, unlike Tampa where I had been rollerblading on a flat surface, this path was nothing I would be able to conquer with my rollerblades. The terrain there was quite hilly and treacherous for someone who only rollerbladed on flat surfaces. I realized this after taking a few spills.

As I mentioned, outside of Columbus is Fort Benning, a U.S. Army post which supports more than 120,000 active military. Outside the entrance to Fort Benning are numerous liquor stores and discount beer outlets. Because of the number of soldiers stationed at Ft. Benning, Columbus always appeared to me to be a youthful city with many young families that I assumed were soldiers and their families living on base.

I would see these young families around town and at the mall. To honor the soldiers from Ft. Benning, every year the Redstixx would have a Military Appreciation Day. On that day, the Redstixx players would wear camouflage jerseys to honor the Military.

It was Labor Day weekend when I attended the scheduled Redstixx doubleheader. Since it was the last home date of the Redstixx season, it was Fan Appreciation Day and they raffled off the camouflage jerseys that the players wore on Military Appreciation Day. I'm happy to say that I won one.

I think it is beautiful and I wear it to baseball games on Memorial Day and 4th of July holiday weekends. I also wear it if I attend a game on September 11th. The game worn jersey had been worn by Sean Swedlow who also autographed it. I got to go on the field and meet him when I went to retrieve the jersey.

Sean told me the players were in a bad mood as the game they just lost had eliminated the Redstixx from the playoffs. Little did he or I know that there would be no minor league playoffs that year.

Sean had been drafted by the Indians in the third round of the 2000 Major League Baseball draft, a pretty high draft choice. He played for three years in the Indians' minor league system and never got above the lower A level before the Indians released him.

As I mentioned above, the lower A level of the minor leagues basically means that there are three levels that a player has to be promoted through before he reaches the major leagues. To show how difficult it is to reach the majors from that lower A level, 52 players wore the Columbus Redstixx jersey in 2001 and only eight of those players appeared in the Major Leagues. Two of those eight were called up once each in September when the rosters expanded.

For me, life was good at the time as I was again in a relationship with a woman in Tampa who I had recently started dating. I know this sounds familiar. Like a previous relationship, I was looking forward to getting back to Tampa. The relationship was in its infancy and she and I had a trip planned to New York City for the weekend of September 21, 2001. Also, she was going to be at the Tampa airport when I arrived back from my trip.

She was not going to be there to pick me up. I had learned my lesson and parked my car at the airport. She would be there picking her brother up from a flight that he was arriving on at about the same time my flight was arriving.

While in Atlanta, I picked up a replica Braves jersey for her. She was there at the airport waiting for me, and unlike a previous girlfriend, she had not found another boyfriend. At least, not yet. It was neat to give the jersey to her when I arrived in Tampa and we talked about the trip we had planned to New York City three weeks later.

However, like the minor league playoffs, that trip would never take place either. The events of 9/11 would rear their ugly head. After September 11th, major league baseball would take a one week hiatus and the minor league playoffs were all cancelled.

When I talked to my friend on September 11th, she said that there was no way she was going to fly anywhere anytime soon. The trip to New York was cancelled and she and I would never travel anywhere. In fact, the relationship started to wane around that time.

It was heart breaking for me. I had not been involved with a woman for a few years before this relationship and it would be a long time before I would spend time with a woman I was attracted to again. In 2001, I had already started to plan to move back to Cleveland but that plan was on hold for a short time as I wanted to see how this relationship worked out.

The relationship that would keep me in Tampa never happened. She and I did spend some time together over the next couple months but the relationship was not to be. The plan to move back to Cleveland started moving toward its fruition.

Obviously, the country was stunned after 9/11. I remember having trouble sleeping that night after the attack thinking that maybe Americans were all now vulnerable to even another attack that we certainly did not expect. In a real irony, the night before 9/11, I was teaching a college success course and a student asked me why people around the world hated us. I don't recall my answer but it certainly was a timely question.

With the New York City trip cancelled, I decided to go out of town anyway. The President wanted us to travel, so I did. I went to Miami to see two Florida Marlins games. The first game was on Friday, September 28th and I saw a great game between the Marlins and the Phillies. Kevin Millar socked a game winning home run in the bottom of the 10th to beat the Phillies 6-5.

A few weeks later, I would fly to Atlanta for a Braves' playoff game. While at the Tampa airport, I recognized an attorney that I knew. He was wearing a camouflage uniform at the airport. He had been called up from the reserve to patrol the airport with other reservists.

CHAPTER FIFTEEN

2012 Season

When the 2012 regular season ended, the Texas Rangers finished in second place in the American League West Division. After leading the American League West by as many as fourteen games during the 2012 season, the Rangers were still five games ahead of the second place Oakland Athletics with nine games left in the season. However, the Oakland A's got hot at the end of the season and swept a three game series in Oakland against the Rangers. That sweep gave the A's the American League West crown.

The Texas Rangers found themselves in the new one game Wild Card playoff hosting the Baltimore Orioles. Much like the upstart Oakland A's, the Orioles were not intimidated by the Rangers' home field advantage and beat the Rangers 5-1.

The loss was a crushing blow to the Rangers' goal of winning a World Series, something they failed to do the previous two seasons when they lost the World Series in 2010 to the San Francisco Giants and to the St. Louis Cardinals in 2011.

All the Rangers players who appeared in the 5th of May game at Progressive Field were still on the Rangers team when the season ended. The same can't be said for the Cleveland Indians players who played that evening.

After the game on May 5th, the Indians were still in first place in the American League Central Division by 1 1/2 games with a 14-11 record. They entered the All-Star break with a 44-41 record in second place behind the first place Chicago White Sox by three games. The Indians were 1/2 game ahead of the third place Detroit Tigers who would eventually go on to win the Central Division.

The second half of the season did not go well for the Indians. They lost all nine games on a road trip from late July and into early August 2012. Their record in August was 5-24.

That performance would lead to the firing of Indians manager, Manny Acta, in late September. He was replaced by bench coach and former Tribe catcher, Sandy Alomar, Jr. His managerial career would last six games as the Indians would hire Terry Francona as their manager after the season ended.

Of the Indians position players that played that night, Michael Brantley, Jason Kipnis, Asdrubal Cabrera, Carlos Santana, Travis Hafner and Shin-Soo Choo, who were the first six batters in the Tribe lineup, all ended the season with the team.

Shelley Duncan, the Indians left fielder, was released from the Indians on August 29, 2012. Johnny Damon, who pinch hit for Duncan, was released by the Indians on August 9th. His time with the Indians may have been the last of his playing career. Third baseman Jack Hannahan and catcher Lou Marson ended the season with the Indians.

Derek Lowe, the Indians starting pitcher, was released by the Indians on August 10th and was signed by the New York Yankees on August 13th and found himself in post-season play. Nick Hagadone, who relieved Lowe, would end up on the disabled list after injuring his hand in what was described as a "self inflicted" injury to his pitching hand. The injury occurred after he gave up two runs in two-thirds of an inning against the Tampa Bay Rays. It is believed that he hit his fist against a wall in a fit of anger afterwards.

The Indians placed Hagadone on the disqualified list which meant the Indians would not have to pay him. Afterward, the Major League Players Association filed a grievance on his behalf against the Indians attempting to get him paid during that time. The other two relief pitchers who pitched that night, Joe Smith and Vinnie Pestano, ended the season with the Indians.

I did get to see post-season baseball. On October 7th, I went to Detroit to see the Tigers beat the Oakland A's 5-4 and take a 2-0 game lead in the best of five American League Division Series. The highlight of that game was when Coco Crisp, the Oakland A's center fielder whose name has already appeared in this book a few times, dropped a line drive that was hit directly to him. His error allowed two Tigers runners to score. The Tigers would go on to win the Division Series over the A's.

The Tigers would go on to win the American League Championship Series over the New York

Yankees and move on to play in the World Series. On Saturday, October 27th, I would attend Game Three of the World Series and watch the Tigers get shutout 2-0 by the San Francisco Giants. The weather was not conducive to baseball as the temperature at game time was 40 degrees and the winds were gusting up to 25 miles per hour. It would get colder.

The Tigers would lose the World Series in just four games to the Giants. It would be four months and twelve days before I would attend another baseball game.

CHAPTER SIXTEEN

Where are they now?

Nancy Shuford Craig, my niece, survived being abandoned by me that night in 1986 and went on to graduate from Boston University in 1987 with a Bachelors Degree in Communications. She and her husband, Mark, now live in Los Angeles. After a successful career in advertising as a brand strategist, she went back to school and graduated with a Masters degree in Spiritual Psychology from the University of Santa Monica in 2004. She now operates her own brand strategy business and works as a life coach in southern California.

Scott Robinson and his family are living in Charleston, West Virginia. On August 2nd, 2013 he was in South Carolina when he learned that they had a heart for him at the Cleveland Clinic. He was flown up immediately and operated on.

I'm ecstatic to tell everyone that he is fine. He was discharged from the Clinic one week after the operation although he had to stay in the Cleveland area for a period of time thereafter. He is on Facebook and hosts a Charleston WV Baseball History page where he regularly posts historical photos of Charleston baseball teams as well as updates of the Pittsburgh Pirates and their minor league teams of which the West Virginia Power is one. His operation went so well that he was in good enough shape to throw out the first pitch at a West Virginia Power playoff game after the 2013 regular season. You can follow Scott's progress on a Facebook page, Prayers for *Scotty D* Robinson.

J.J. Pearsall, the pitcher for the Savannah Sand Gnats that I met in 1996, lives in Nassau, New York near Albany. He works for Rensselaer County as a GIS technician. He still plays baseball in the Albany Twilight League for the Albany Athletics and in 2012 became the oldest player (at the ripe old age of 38) to win the league's Pitcher of the Year award. His team also won the Stan Musial World Series in 2012. The Stan Musial World Series is operated by the American Amateur Baseball Congress and is for teams with amateur players of any age.

Carla Caillier, the woman I represented who received the death penalty that was later reduced to life imprisonment, is still in prison. Florida Department of Correction records show that she is in the Lowell Correctional Institution in Ocala, Florida. Since being imprisoned, she was also convicted of Conspiracy to Commit Escape and Constructive Possession of Contraband in 1992. She was sentenced to four years in prison to run concurrently with her life imprisonment.

Since she has a life sentence with no possibility of parole for at least 25 years, I believe the practical effect of the four year sentence is that it adds four years to the time she would be eligible for parole which would now be sometime in 2016. Gilbert Hadas was the prison minister who sneaked wire cutters and hacksaw blades to her after professing his love to her and his desire to help her escape. It was alleged that he had gone so far as to consider using a helicopter to pluck her out of the prison. He received a one month jail sentence, 300 hours of community service and four years of probation for the same crimes that Carla was convicted of.

Everett Pearsall, my Dad, passed away in June 2000. He was 84 years old and still lived in his home on Lake Erie in Lorain, Ohio when he passed away. He was retired after working his whole life for Fruehauf Trailer Company. Although we were not real close and did not share many similar interests, I look back and appreciate the fact that he got up every morning, went to work and made sure that his children were taken care of. He did die when I had a baseball trip scheduled. I did cancel my baseball trip.

Bernice Pearsall, my Mom, passed away in 2011 in a nursing home in Westlake, Ohio. She was 89 and spent most of her last three years in the nursing home. I was happy that I moved back from Tampa in 2003 to spend time with her, help her and be with her until the time she passed away.

She would kid me by telling me that she thought the real reason I moved back to Cleveland was so I could see more Indians games. While she was in the nursing home, she was still able to play piano without having to read music. I made her especially happy when I played the piano for her. I started playing the piano again after she was in the nursing home. It was all there was to do when I was checking on her house in Lorain while doing my laundry there.

The two women who I had just started dating when I took two of the trips I talk about in the book went on to get married. I have lost track of them. The woman I was dating when I went to New York City with my niece also went on to marry and have four children. I did run into her at a Devil Rays game. She was working a concession stand as the Devil Rays allowed nonprofit groups to operate some stands and keep some of the proceeds for the nonprofit group.

I did date a few women when I lived in Tampa and actually lived with a woman........when baseball was on strike in 1994.

Finally, early in this book I mentioned a case in which I represented the owner of an ostrich that was frightened by the noise made by an ascending hot air balloon. The frightened ostrich ran back and forth in its pen and broke a leg and had to be put down. That case was settled out of court.